THE BOOMERS' GUIDEBOOK TO MORE JOYOUS LIVING

Twenty Positive Approaches to Life after Fifty

BY

DR. DON WEINHOUSE

ISBN: 1490433740

ISBN 13: 9781490433745

Library of Congress Control Number: 2013911314
CreateSpace Independent Publishing Platform
North Charleston, South Carolina

TABLE OF CONTENTS

Acknowledgments

When I was five or six years old, I often played with a neighbor child who was not a pleasant person to be around. I can't remember his name or specific things he did that I didn't like. What I do remember is that sometime during kindergarten or first grade I made a conscious decision, a great decision, a life-shaping decision to stay away—as much as possible—from him and anyone else I didn't like or respect. I want to thank that unnamed boy because ever since that time, I've done a great job selecting friends, role models, and mentors.

I want to acknowledge specifically the number one, best, most incredible friend/role model/mentor I've learned from and with in my life—my wife and partner, Marilyn. Thank you for sharing this long and wonderful journey with me and for helping me discover myself and the "twenty positive approaches to life after fifty." And in advance, thank you for helping me begin the search for "twenty more positive approaches to life after seventy," which I sense we've already begun the groundwork for.

Another special shout-out to my daughter, Rachel. You were and are a great resource, catalyst, and test site for my understanding of and progress in all areas but especially relating to the chapters on feeling, loving, playing, celebration, negotiating, influencing, and giving. Way to go, girl!

I also want to acknowledge the editors at CreateSpace. Many thanks for making the manuscript adhere to the rules of English, something I so often neglect to do.

FOREWORD

By Marilyn Morse Weinhouse

If anyone is qualified to write a self-help book, it is Don. He lives each and every concept presented in this book, and I can honestly say he is the most joyful person I have ever known.

I met Don in 1976...and married him in 1976. Sometimes you just know! Don was, and is, one of the most amazing people I have ever met. I was drawn to his openness, honesty, humor, and intense focus on developing spiritually.

Don is unique in so many ways! First and foremost is the level of *joy* he experiences daily. He wakes each morning with a smile on his face, full of energy and enthusiasm. He appreciates every person he meets, every place he visits, and every situation he encounters. When hardships come his way, he faces them with the faith that "Whatever is, is right...and everything will be fine in the end."

Another unique quality that continues to amaze me, even after all these years, is Don's extraordinary level of self-discipline. He rarely talks about it, and I wouldn't believe it if I hadn't seen it with my own eyes, day after day after day. Don rises early (usually at 3:00 or 4:00 a.m.) *every* day to stretch, do yoga, and meditate. Do you see that word *every*? Don also exercises every day and regularly makes time for his hobbies of juggling and playing the flute and recorder.

Don is an adventurer. His love of life combined with his love of new experiences has led him on many exciting journeys (dragging me along on most of them ☺)—traveling throughout India, Thailand, Nepal, China, Southeast Asia, and Europe; living and working in Taiwan and Japan; practicing his hobbies at yoga ashrams and international juggling festivals.

I can't fully describe Don without also mentioning his playfulness and sense of humor. Children and the young-at-heart are drawn to him like a magnet, as he is so fun loving and lives in the moment. Lest I give a false impression of a happy-go-lucky guy, I will add that he experiences his emotions deeply and cries easily (and frequently) over both joyous occasions and sorrowful situations.

And last, as Don's wife, I must add that he has been a remarkable father to our daughter, Rachel. He has been involved in her growth and development since day one, and now that she is an adult, he continues to provide loving support and guidance. Don's ideas about parenting have helped make Rachel the exceptional person she is today and have helped the many parents and teachers he has encountered in his teaching career and through his conference presentations and books *Little Children, Big Needs* (1994) and *Encouraging Potential in Young Children* (1998).

I hope the ideas in *The Boomers' Guidebook to More Joyous Living* provide you with strategies to create a more joyous and fulfilling life.

INTRODUCTION

Hi. Don here. (Some say boomers have a tendency to behave a bit too familiarly.) I'm the author of *The Boomers' Guidebook to More Joyous Living*. During my career as a teacher, principal, and university professor, I was usually introduced as Dr. Don, or Professor Weinhouse, but that was years ago, before my first retirement, in the days when I was more defined by position, degrees, and professional accomplishments. You might be able to relate to that, to a changing definition of who you are. Because changing we are!

I wrote this book for myself (some say boomers tend to be egocentric) and my eighty million North American brothers and sisters (some say boomers are, population-wise, "the pig in the python") who feel they are pushing— or perhaps have broken past—middle age.

I wrote this book because, after thirty-five years of motivated, caring, I-can-change-the-world, career-focused, achievement-oriented work (some say boomers should be referred to as the "workaholic generation"), I found I really didn't have to or want to be involved in my career full time anymore and wasn't very motivated to achieve a higher position or gain more status.

I wrote this book because, like many boomers, I feel good about where the past decades have brought me and want to share the positive approaches to life I've employed to get me to this place—positive approaches you might wish to consider incorporating into your own life. (Some say boomers are a confident and self-reliant generation.)

There's a very good chance you're already familiar with many of the twenty approaches discussed in the following pages. Great! Read those chapters, celebrate your efforts, have a look at the topic from a different perspective, and keep it up. There's also a good chance you've considered a number of other approaches but haven't really run with them yet. Fine! Give them another look and consider whether the time might not be right to do a bit more work in that area. Regarding approaches that don't appeal to you, I recommend that you put them aside for a few months or years and perhaps consider them again someday—one size does not fit all on the path to personal growth. (Some say boomers are independent and questioning.)

The Boomers' Guidebook was written to help you reflect on who you are and where you're going and to provide some starting points for furthering this investigation. It's a guidebook to lifelong adventures you yourself can create.

Even though each section is small, the ideas are big, so I recommend that you take time to reflect on each topic, each quotation, and each story.

Those quotations and stories found throughout the book that are not attributed to specific individuals are compilations and paraphrases derived from the experiences and stories of the many hundreds of real people I have met and spoken with over the past decades.

CHAPTER 1

PLAY JUST FOR THE FUN OF IT

"We don't stop playing because we grow old;
we grow old because we stop playing."
George Bernard Shaw,
early nineteenth-century British playwright

Why is PLAYING important?

Play is fun, anxiety-free, engaging, stress-reducing, and energizing. It offers a connection with the joyous child within, provides a temporary respite from distracting thoughts and concerns, and creates a bond with others. Work, study, contemplation, and fulfilling commitments are all important, but they aren't everything. Wake up.

Get dressed. Eat meals. Pay bills. Go to sleep. Day in and day out. Year in and year out. Put them all together, and without play, life can become drudgery, predictable and boring.

As a group, playful individuals have stronger immune systems, a lower incidence of psychosomatic ailments, and more positive outlooks on life. They live longer and are less likely to become drug- or alcohol-dependent. Play is the wonder drug—noncarcinogenic, powerful, inexpensive, and easy to engage in alone or with others.

> "Our minds need relaxation, and give way
> Unless we mix with work a little play."
> **Moliere, seventeenth-century French comedy writer**

How to PLAY

The pleasure derived from play doesn't have to come with smiles or laughter or be accompanied by any outward expressions. What it does have to do is alter mind and body by pulling you into the moment, a moment that is alive and fresh.

The first task is to identify activities that yield this feeling of pleasure. It's possible that an activity you once avoided might now suit you better. (*I never played cards when I was younger. I thought it was a waste of time, but now I love it!*) It's also possible that an activity that once brought you pleasure no longer does. (*I used to play a lot of tennis. I loved hitting the ball around and often didn't even keep score. It's not the same anymore. I can't safely run, or stop fast, or cut from side to side like I used to, and just standing there and hitting the ball doesn't do it for me.*)

In addition to pleasure, play ideally evokes a feeling of freedom—freedom to feel, to experiment with new ways, new ideas, new movements, and new combinations. Without this spontaneity, play can become more habit or ritual and lose some of its power to revitalize and excite.

One thing I love about cooking is the freedom to explore new ideas and combinations. I'm like the captain or conductor of whatever I'm creating, and I can take it anywhere I want to go.

I used to love puttering around in the garden, but the last few months it seems more like a chore. I think I need to get away from it for a while.

> "When we do what we are meant to do...
> the work we do feels like play to us."
> **Julia Cameron, artist and author**

Experiencing and experimenting with your voice or a musical instrument or moving your body or mind in a game can be play if you allow yourself the freedom to explore, change, invent, and flow—if the activity is disassociated from a preconceived, definite product.

Practicing a piece of music, trying to perform it exactly as written, isn't play. It's practice. Practice places limits on an activity that play doesn't. Practice diminishes the free, open, creative, in-the-moment aspects of the music, the process, in favor of the sought-after product. Practice can be enjoyable, is most certainly necessary to improve performance, and can occur side-by-side with play, but practice isn't play.

Competition, like practice, may include elements of play; however, an individual's competitive edge is threatened by the addition of too much play. Ballroom dance partners who joyously and spontaneously add new, unrehearsed moves during a competition are less likely to go home with a ribbon. The senior league basketball player who experiments with under-the-leg dribbling and behind-the-back passes during the championship game will certainly experience the wrath of teammates. And the chess player who wants to experiment with how well her queen can do without help from knights, castles, or bishops may experience a quick defeat.

> "Live like you'll die tomorrow, work like you don't need the money, and dance like nobody is watching."
>
> **Bob Fosse, Broadway choreographer, performer, and director**

The joy and freedom experienced in play are engaging, expanding, and renewing, and should be experienced often. Don't save play for the right time, or until the weekend, or for when the grandkids are in town. Take advantage of opportunities whenever and wherever they may arise.

*Enviously observing the neighbor kids throwing a ball around? Why not ask to join in?

*Love doing crossword puzzles on airplane flights and during vacations? Why not take a few minutes from your regular schedule to engage in the activity?

*Walking on a beach, reminiscing about how, as a child, you loved skipping rocks? Why not skip a few?

Play is similar to appreciating a sunset, rainbow, or embrace from a loved one—when the opportunity presents itself, take it!

> "Play is our brain's favorite way of learning."
> **Diane Ackerman, MA, MFA, PhD, poet, counselor, and teacher**

Examples of PLAYING

Frannie describes her sister with pride.

My older sister, Ruth, is one of those people everyone loves to be around. She's kind and respectful and can be serious when she wants, but she loves playing with words. She twists them, turns them, uses them in funny, unique ways, speaks with different accents, and basically has a ball. Sometimes she does get a bit wired or fired up and has a little trouble slowing down, but I've never seen her word games hurt or offend anyone. She was a successful businesswoman and has a great family life and loads of friends, yet still acts like the playful kid I grew up with.

Jeff, a fifty-nine-year-old salesman reminisces about his early love of skateboarding.

I used to ride my skateboard everywhere. From the age of six to twenty, I never left home without one. I never skateboard anymore—haven't in decades—but every chance I get I play with my sense of balance by walking along the side of curbs, doing different yoga positions that require balance, riding bicycles with no hands, and all sorts of other lame ideas that usually annoy my wife. Just thirty seconds climbing over boulders at the park or gliding across the supermarket parking lot on the back of a shopping cart, and I feel the same rush and excitement I did when I was a kid.

"Play keeps us vital and alive.
It gives us an enthusiasm for life that is irreplaceable."
Lucia Capocchione, writer, art therapist, and consultant

Sixty-eight-year-old Ellen and her husband are still playing.

When my husband and I were younger, we went scuba diving and snorkeling around the world, played competitive tennis, backpacked throughout the Rockies, and skied the most difficult runs we could find. With age and injuries, we've cut back on many of those activities, but one thing we've kept up with, and are more into than ever, is dancing. Twice a week we ballroom dance and usually do swing or salsa once a week. We may not be young anymore, but we still have the moves. When we get out on that floor, it's like we're floating on a cloud. We're so into holding each other and gliding around the dance floor, moving this way and that, trying new things, and having fun, the time just flies by.

"If A is success in life, then A equals
x plus y plus z.
Work is x; y is play; and z is
keeping your mouth shut."
**Albert Einstein, world-renowned scientist and father
of the theory of relativity theory**

Review

Play **alone or with others**, with **freedom** and **creativity,without concern about the product** of your play.

✻

Self-Reflection

Consider your three favorite *play* activities in regards to how well they provide you with freedom, creative expression, and the opportunity to be engaged without concern for the products of your play.

Chapter 2

BREATHE Deeply and Attentively

Why is BREATHING important?

Deep, slow, focused breathing is relaxing, increases oxygen flow to the brain, slows the heart rate, and lowers blood pressure.

Focusing on the breath can help disengage your mind from the energy-draining mental-rehashing and interpreting of past events and protect you from becoming overwhelmed by to-do lists and future concerns.

As your breathing becomes slower and deeper, sensory experiences are heightened: the breeze that brushes your cheek brings a greater sense of delight; the warmth of a handshake or hug carries a clearer message; and the smell of a wood-burning fire more dramatically refreshes memories and emotions long forgotten.

> "Each breath is a gift. So breathe deeply."
> **Golda Meir, prime minister of Israel (1969–1974)**

How to BREATHE

Although breathing air, like digesting food, pumping blood, and sweating, is an automatic body function, it is also one you have some control over. You can improve the quality of your breathing and use your inhalations and exhalations to alter your mental, physical, and spiritual states.

Improved breathing begins with paying more attention to the breath as it passes in and out. Observe its flow: in... out...in...out. Feel the air. Follow its movement as it moves into your nose and throughout your body, and then notice as it reverses its path and exits through your nose.

Substantial medical research as well as centuries-old yoga practices favor breathing through the nose whenever possible. However, slow, long, deep breathing through the mouth, or through the nose and mouth simultaneously, is beneficial as well.

These are the most important points to remember: entry and exit points—NOSE; depth—DEEP; speed—SLOW; and focus—CALMLY OBSERVING.

> "Your breathing determines whether you are at your best
> or whether you are at a disadvantage."
> **Carola Speads, author and health consultant**

Nice and slow. In-in-in. Hold-hold-hold. Out-out-out. Wait-wait-wait. In-in-in. Hold-hold-hold. Out-out-out. Wait-wait-wait. Follow the air as it enters. Hold it in your expanded diaphragm. Release it as your diaphragm contracts. Wait. Enjoy the emptiness.

When you become aware that your mind has drifted from the breath to a thought, come back to the breath. When the mind drifts off again, come back again. Again and again and again and again, come back to the breath. This simple exercise will almost immediately spread its benefits as you find yourself calmer, more connected with your body, and more in tune with others and the surrounding environment.

If you find it difficult to follow your breath attentively, experiment with one of the following approaches:

*Mentally repeat *in-hold-out-wait...in-hold-out-wait... in-hold-out-wait.* Think *in* as you breathe in, hold as you hold the air in your lungs, *out as you release the air, and wait as you briefly enjoy the emptiness.*

*Listen to and mentally repeat the sound, as you hear or perceive it, emanating from your nostrils (perhaps *ahh* during the inhalation and *eee* during exhalation).

*Experience the coolness of each breath as you inhale and the warmth when exhaling.

*Silently, recite this to yourself: *In 1-2-3-4-5. Pause. Out 1-2-3-4-5. Pause. In 1-2-3-4-5. Pause. Out 1-2-3-4-5. Pause.* Gradually lengthen the count as you are able.

The effects of calm, controlled breathing range from soothing anxiety and alleviating pain to enhancing energy and creating an overall sense of well-being.

Breathing has helped me a lot with some bad thoughts I fall prey to. As soon as I become aware that I'm drifting into one of my negative, mental broken-records, I do one of a number of breathing exercises and most often pull myself out.

I focus on my breath when I speed-walk and jog. Attentive breathing gives me more physical and mental energy and also seems to get the endorphins going faster and stronger.

I listen to the sound of the air coming in and going out of my nose when I'm weaving. It brings me more in touch with what I'm doing and heightens my senses.

Specific breathing techniques are useful, but the one, most important approach is to *be more aware* as you inhale and exhale deep, slow breaths through your nose.

> "No matter how much pressure you
> feel at work,
> if you could find ways to relax for at least five
> minutes every hour,
> you'd be more productive."
> **Dr. Joyce Brothers, psychologist, author, and TV/**
> **radio personality**

Examples of BREATHING

Simon suffers from a mild case of social anxiety.

I sat there at my parents' sixtieth-anniversary party, frozen. Every time I tried to enter into one of the little groups of chatting relatives, my mind jumped to thoughts like, "I can't do it," and "I know I'm going to embarrass myself." Then, I remembered a technique my counselor recommended a couple of weeks ago. I breathed in and felt the coolness of the air in my nose, breathed out and felt the warmth. I did this over and over and over again. In a few seconds, I started feeling calmer. After a minute or two, I was taking longer breaths, the negative thoughts stopped, and I felt my heart rate slow. Feeling relaxed and comfortable, I really connected with a couple of cousins I hadn't talked to in years.

> "Fear is excitement without the breath."
> **Fritz Perls, MD, psychiatrist, author, and father of Gestalt Psychotherapy**

Heather, a sixty-one-year-old pediatrician, finds walking calming.

I love walking in nature. When I get out of work early, l drive to this park I like and just start walking. Sometimes, if my mind is busy with patient or family issues, I'll walk for twenty minutes before I even realize I'm doing more worrying than walking. When I become aware this is going on, I silently begin counting the rhythm of my breath. I count to five or ten as I inhale, hold the air for a few seconds, count to five or ten as I exhale, enjoy the emptiness for a few seconds, and repeat the process over and over again. Usually, within a very few minutes I become aware of the birds singing, sunlight streaming through the leaves, and all the wonderful smells.

> "Breathing is the first place, not the last, one should look when fatigue, disease, or other evidence of disordered energy presents itself."
> **Sheldon Saul Hendler, PhD, MD, professor of medicine and author**

Jack, a mortgage banker in his late sixties, admits that he's not always a good listener.

The other day I was having lunch with my son. He was talking, and I was mostly listening, but my mind kept wandering to stuff like, "Did I mail the auto insurance check?" "I really need to have my tires rotated." "Should I have dessert?" All of a sudden, one word brought me back to the conversation. DIVORCE. I pulled in a deep breath of air, dropped all other thoughts from my consciousness, and asked, "Did you say 'divorce'?" For the next twenty minutes, to help me concentrate on his concerns and cut all the other stuff out of my head, I drew in long, deep breaths of air and felt my body as it expanded and contracted.

"The best things in life are nearest...
Breath in your nostrils, light in your eyes,
flowers at your feet..."
**Robert Louis Stevenson, nineteenth-century
Scottish author**

Review

Breathe **deeply, slowly,** and **attentively through the nose.**

✻

Self-Reflection

Take the next two or three minutes and *breathe* deeply, slowly, and attentively through your nose. Then remain in that position for a short time and take an inventory of how your body and mind feel.

CHAPTER 3

MEDITATE IN WAYS
THAT BRING PEACE

"Learn to get in touch with the silence within yourself
and know that everything in this life has a purpose."
Elizabeth Kubler-Ross, MD, psychiatrist, and author
of the groundbreaking book *On Death and Dying*

Why is MEDITATING important?

Much like breathing, meditation is an easy, free, enjoyable,
time-efficient way to relax the body, rejuvenate the spirit,
cleanse the mind, and restore attention and energy that
may have been diminished through normal, day-to-day
interactions with life.

When your mind is distracted by thoughts unrelated to your present physical surroundings, you too easily miss potentially enjoyable, educational, enriching, and revitalizing experiences. How many times have you not fully appreciated a beautiful scene because your awareness was shrouded in anxiety over some future possibility? How often has a person you love shared something important, but the communication was lost as you drifted in thoughts of yesterday or tomorrow? Meditation can help you become more calm and focused, bring you back to the here and now, and reveal deeper levels of yourself buried beneath the storm of crashing thoughts.

> "Not only a truer knowledge, but a greater power comes to one in the quietude and silence of a mind that, instead of bubbling on the surface, can go to its own depths and listen."
> **Sri Aurobindo, twentieth-century Indian yogi and spiritual leader**

How to MEDITATE

It's possible to meditate standing, sitting, lying down, walking, jogging, swimming, skiing, or skating...eyes opened or closed, in a group or alone, in the midst of noise or absolute silence...for five seconds, five minutes, or five hours. The focus of meditation may be silence, or a sound, phrase, sentence, color, mental picture, emotion, or breath. The common factor in this vast array of options, the essence of meditation, is returning to the technique when you become aware that your mind has drifted away from it.

The most often taught form of meditation is seated, with eyes closed. Seated, eyes-closed meditation is typically accomplished in a quiet setting where one is able to capture at least fifteen to twenty minutes of undisturbed solitude. Meditation texts and teachers suggest practitioners sit straight and tall with feet on the ground. You can meditate while reclining or lying down, of course, but meditations in these postures often turn into naps. Napping is also beneficial and recharging but doesn't possess the same long-term, mind-altering effects as meditation—it doesn't as reliably enhance your ability to connect with deeper levels of consciousness lying beneath the stream of thoughts.

> "The truth that sets us free is an embrace of the divine within us."
> **Marianne Williamson, contemporary American lecturer and writer**

With eyes closed, listen to and feel your breath as it enters and exits the nostrils. Breathe slowly and deeply. As discussed in the previous chapter, simply observing the breathing process can be a powerfully relaxing and rejuvenating form of meditation. However, once the breath deepens and slows, and the mind is calmer, there is a wide variety of other meditation techniques available.

*Mentally, silently repeat a relaxing word or mantra. (*Om,* pronounced "aum," and other Sanskrit mantras are commonly used.)

*Envision a field of wheat swaying in the wind, clouds floating through one another, a bright sun shining in a blue sky, a waterfall, or any similarly tranquil image.

*Focus attention just below the center of the forehead (the "third eye").

*Silently repeat a short prayer or positive affirmation, such as the Lord's Prayer, the Hebrew Shema, or a phrase like "We are all one," or "Peace surrounds me."

All are different forms of meditation. All are rejuvenating. And all can bring you more in touch with the moment and your higher self.

> "Prayer is when you talk to God; meditation is when you listen to God."
> **Diana Robinson, PhD, author, and personal effectiveness coach**

When you become aware that a random thought has invaded your meditation (*I need to get a haircut...my neck feels tense...as soon as I finish this meditation, I have to call Frank*), briefly acknowledge it and then return to the focus of the meditation, whether that is a mantra, visual image, or a phrase. If you fall asleep and are awakened by the whiplash sensation of your chin dropping to chest, gently bring your attention back to the meditation.

Once these techniques become easier and more natural, many can be practiced with eyes open, while standing, knitting, walking, cooking, or whatever mundane task you are employed in.

*While waiting in a long line, drop the worry and anxiety over your daughter's difficult pregnancy or tomorrow's yearly oncology checkup and replace it with a

MEDITATE IN WAYS THAT BRING PEACE   21

mantra, or calming thought, repeated over and over again, or the smiling image of a beloved, distant, or deceased relative, or...

*When out on a walk, disengage from the mental calculations of how much each house or car you pass might cost and instead focus on the beating of your heart or the rhythm of your footsteps or...

Two ideal times for seated, eyes-closed meditation are in the morning soon after arising and in the afternoon before dinner. And you can do a shorter, eyes-open meditation any time during the day when you have a free moment or two and don't need your full attention for the activity you're involved in.

The key is doing it. Find the time. Find the place. And make it an everyday part of life.

> "When meditation works as it should, it will be a natural part of your being."
> **Ram Dass, twentieth-century American psychologist, author, and spiritual guide**

Examples of MEDITATING

Tatum, a sixty-two-year-old waitress, proudly proclaims her commitment to meditation.

I've been meditating for over thirty years. I started with Transcendental Meditation—silently repeating a Sanskrit sound in my mind—and then did a type of visual meditation, focusing on colors. For the past ten years, I've been doing my own combination of the two systems. At first, the hardest part for me was finding twenty minutes, twice a day, when I could sit quietly, alone, and not be disturbed. I worked it out in the mornings by waking up before anyone else in the house. In the afternoons, I park on a quiet side street on my way home from work and meditate in the car. I can't tell you exactly what I've gained from meditating, but I can tell you my life is getting better and better.

"He who conquers the mind, conquers the world."
Paramahansa Yogananda, Indian yogi, author, and founder of the Self-Realization Fellowship

---

Curtis, a pediatric dentist, passionately exclaims,

Before I started meditating, I wasn't aware of how daydreamy and time-wasting I was. But the first time I sat down and tried to focus on the sound "OM," I realized my attention was like a tornado, unpredictably and frequently changing direction. I'm guessing my brain has spent about 90 percent of its life haphazardly bouncing around from one random thought to another. It's not like I'm a master meditator or anything, but at least now I'm aware that I can take charge of what I'm thinking about. I can calm and focus myself more.

Shannon has been meditating for many years but only recently figured out a way to use it to help deal with a challenge she's been experiencing.

I used to sleep like a log. I'd lie down, close my eyes, and that would be it, sayonara. However, last year I turned fifty, started menopause, and began waking up in the middle of the night with hot flashes. I didn't want to take any medication and decided to use meditation to help me. If I can't fall asleep, I prop some pillows behind me, sit up, and picture myself seated on a mountaintop, surrounded by snow. Just like in my regular meditations, as soon as I'm aware that my attention has drifted off, I gently move back to the picture in my mind of me, sitting in the snow. About 80 percent of the time I do this, within ten minutes I slide back under the covers and fall into a deep sleep. Maybe it's not "real meditation," but it works!

"Reading makes a full man, meditation a profound man, discourse a clear man."
Benjamin Franklin, eighteenth-century inventor and one of the founding fathers of the United States

---

Review

Meditate by mentally **focusing on the breath and/ or a word, mantra, visual picture, or brief, uplifting thought**, and **returning there once you realize your mind has wandered.**

✺

Self-Reflection

Sit up straight and tall, close your eyes, and for the next five minutes focus attention on the center of your forehead while thinking the sound om/aum.

How did that work for you?

CHAPTER 4

EXERCISE THROUGHOUT EACH DAY

"Physical fitness is not only one of the most
important keys to a healthy body,
it is the basis of dynamic and creative
intellectual activity."
John F. Kennedy, thirty-fifth president
of the United States

Why is EXERCISING important?

One person, one body. Spare parts sometimes available, but replacement often expensive, always painful, and rarely as reliable as the original.

Exercise can help you

*warm up your muscles and joints in the morning, which can help you face the day with more flexibility, energy, and clarity of thought;

*keep your muscles well toned so you can expect more strength and endurance, which can allow you the opportunity to engage in a wider variety of activities for a longer period of time;

*maintain a reasonable weight and experience more pleasurable digestion, greater ease in movement, increased vitality, and less strain, injury, and eventual breakdown in ankles, knees, hips, back, and heart; and

*practice good posture and foster stronger back and neck muscles, a better flow of energy through the spine and brain stem, and a more confident and healthy appearance.

In addition, if you stretch before bed, you can spend less time trying to fall asleep, and diminished stiffness or discomfort upon arising. Exercise throughout each day, and you'll enjoy a great opportunity to slow the aging process, clear the mind of excess baggage, and live better and longer.

Who you are if you exercise is very different from who you are if you don't.

"The higher your energy level, the more efficient your body.
The more efficient your body, the better you feel and the more you will use your talent to produce outstanding results."
Anthony Robbins, motivational author and speaker

How to EXERCISE

Your body, like an automobile, should be allowed a little time to warm up before significant demands are made on it. Soon after rising from an evening's sleep, a few minutes dedicated to exercises like the following would be highly beneficial:

*Slowly and carefully stretch hands to the sky, over-head, from side to side, and down toward the floor.

*Sit with legs outstretched and bend forward, moving hands gently toward ankles and feet.

*Lie on your back, pull knees toward chest, and roll from side to side and front to back.

The feelings derived from stretching should be plea-surable, not painful. Ease up or slow down if you experi-ence pain or discomfort. Hold each position for at least ten to fifteen seconds, slowly return to the starting position, and repeat the movement. Any gentle stretch you design is appropriate, as long as there's little or no pain and you feel a soothing extension of your muscles.

The most important body parts to work on are those that limit your movement or cause pain or discomfort.

*Tight neck? Move your right ear toward the right shoulder and left to left; chin to chest then forehead back, toward the sky; body straight, turn head as if looking behind the left shoulder, then right—always slowly and holding the final position for at least ten to fifteen seconds.

*Painful lower back? Hands on waist, feet and legs unmoving, make small circles from the waist; stand facing a wall, place palms against the wall, and slowly slide hands higher and higher.

"Use it or lose it."
Jimmy Connors, tennis champion and member of the Tennis Hall of Fame, ranked number one in the world from 1974–1978

Once your body is stretched out and warmed up, you're ready to begin activity.

Life abounds with opportunities to walk, climb stairs, bend, squat, reach, and move in a thousand enjoyable and health-enhancing ways, without changing into workout clothes, taking time from busy schedules, or purchasing special equipment.

*Sitting up straight and tall in a chair improves posture and strengthens back and neck muscles.

*Alternately tensing and relaxing hands, feet, neck, back, stomach, or legs tones muscles and relieves stress and strain.

*Even a small movement like rising onto your toes and coming down strengthens calf muscles and enhances balance.

> ## "Of all exercise, walking is the best."
> **Thomas Jefferson, author of the Declaration of Independence and third president of the United States**

Building different forms of exercise directly into your daily schedule circumvents the common complaint that there's not enough time. The more you look for chances to use your body, the more you'll find them. Take the stairs instead of the elevator. Do sit-ups while watching TV. Walk the dog a bit longer and faster than usual.

You don't need a track, swimming pool, or gym; however, traditional, change-your-outfit-and-get-the-heart-going-and-the-body-sweating exercise is also very beneficial. Cardiovascular exercise leads to a healthier heart, more energy, and a longer life.

Beginning with the quick and easy exercises described above will increase the chances you'll develop the motivation and find the time and energy to jump into the pool and swim laps, lace up your jogging shoes and go for a quick walk or run, or join an exercise class.

Exercise needs to become a priority. Rather than trying to fit it in, exercise is important enough to be a key component of each day, around which other important events and responsibilities are scheduled.

Before climbing into bed, treat muscles, tendons, ligaments, and joints to two or five or ten minutes of stretching—just as you did at the beginning of your day, but now for different reasons. Stretch and reward your body for moving you about all day. Stretch and prepare your body for hours of inactivity. Stretch, breathe, relax, and clear your mind. You'll fall asleep more quickly once the lights go out.

> "You can't store physical fitness, so you've got to work activity into every week of your life."
> **Jacki Sorensen, author and originator**
> **of aerobic dancing**

Examples of EXERCISING

Stewart, a sixty-three-year-old contractor, used to have back trouble.

> *I started having trouble with my back in my late thir-ties, but for the past twenty or more years, it's been fine. When I wake up, I immediately do some light warm-up stretching and basic yoga postures for a few minutes. Almost every lunch hour, I speed walk or go to the gym to swim laps or to spend half an hour on the treadmill. On weekends, my wife and I take long bi-cycle rides or go on hikes. Every evening I go through the same light warm-up stretching and basic yoga ex-ercises I do in the morning. When I was younger, I loved jogging, basketball, football, and handball, but as my back got worse and worse, I figured it was time to change my activities. I love the different kinds of ex-ercise I get now, feel in tune with my body, and know what I need to do to take care of myself.*

Kimiko presently carries 163 pounds on her five-foot-five-inch frame.

Throughout my twenties and thirties, I was in great shape and never weighed more than 120 or 125 pounds. Around forty, I started a steady climb of about three or four pounds a year. Three months ago, I turned fifty-five and broke the 180-pound barrier, all in the same week. That's when I decided enough was enough. Besides cutting down on snacks and eating smaller portions at each meal, I've begun using my body more. I do calf raises in the grocery store checkout line; while on the phone, I do deep knee bends with my back up against a wall; I take the stairs instead of elevators or escalators; and I walk or jog in place or do sit-ups or crunches, when I'm watching TV. I've lost seventeen pounds so far and feel ten years younger.

> "Nothing lifts me out of a bad mood better than a hard workout on my treadmill. It never fails...exercise is nothing short of a miracle."
> **Cher, singer, actress, and fitness consultant**

Randy is a bright and energetic seventy-year-old who, over the past eight years, has had two knee surgeries, two hip replacements, and three months of chemotherapy.

Over the past few years, my favorite exercise tools have been the therapy pool, my stretching/yoga mat, and any chair I'm sitting on. I've learned and created dozens of pool and isometric chair exercises, and safe stretching and yoga postures. They keep me in good shape, and they're fun. I hope to someday get back into golf, tennis, and bowling, but I'm not just sitting around waiting. I'd go nuts if I didn't keep active, not to mention the fact that I love to feel my muscles and heart working hard.

"Health is the vital principle of bliss, and exercise, of health."

James Thomson, nineteenth-century Scottish poet

Review

Gently **exercise as you arise, throughout the day**, and **before you sleep**.

❈

Self-Reflection

What aspects of your *exercise* routine are working well, and what changes are you considering?

Chapter 5

Celebrate Events, Both Large and Small

"When it's a good time, I celebrate. When it's a bad time I also celebrate.
Know what I mean?"
Goldie Hawn, actress, comedian, and author

Why is CELEBRATING important?

Celebrating brings more clearly and intensely to our awareness that which is beautiful, positive, and good in our lives. It creates a momentum that leads to acknowledging a wider array of experiences to delight in. The more you celebrate, the more you find opportunities to celebrate.

Celebrating the many positive, little events that occur in daily life—your grandchild balancing on a bicycle for the first time; the smell and sizzle of burgers on the grill; your bare foot escaping contact with the broken bottle lying half-hidden in the sand—brings more joy into your moment-to-moment existence.

> "Rejoice, lest pleasureless you die."
> **William Morse, nineteenth-century author of** *The Earthly Paradise*

Celebrating the less frequent, significant major events—birthdays, graduations, anniversaries, retirements—ensures that efforts and achievements are acknowledged and rewarded and provides motivation for further accomplishments.

It's sometimes difficult to imagine achieving far-off goals, but when successes are celebrated along the way, you encourage and remind yourself and others that progress is being made. This makes the process seem easier and the goal feel closer.

How to CELEBRATE

You're no doubt already well aware of the many and varied ways in which major life events can be celebrated: mail cards and announcements to family and friends, have a party, take a trip, buy a present, go out for a nice dinner or night on the town. These celebrations are fine. They're great! Enjoying some sort of ritual at life's milestones or upon a major achievement is a well-established and wonderful tradition. However, the celebration of smaller, daily events is also important.

Occasions to celebrate major events may be few and far between, but each and every hour of every day presents many opportunities to rejoice. Be glad your body has the strength and vitality to lift you out of bed; delight in the cold, clear, drinkable water flowing from the faucet; linger in the sense of accomplishment you feel as you feast your eyes on the stacks of clean, folded laundry; and appreciate the less-than-usual traffic that allowed you to arrive home ten minutes early. Grabbing hold of these numerous, everyday pleasures is sustaining, nourishing, fun, and in no way diminishes the recognition and appreciation of big events.

Honey, I slept straight through the night, Judith sang out as she reached her hands toward the ceiling, a smile stretching across her face.

*Raul lifted his thirteen-month-old granddaughter into the air and showered her with hugs and kisses after the toddler successfully walked from the couch to the chair.

*Rhonda bowed her head and whispered a silent prayer of thanks the moment she became aware the back discomfort she had been experiencing for days had subsided.

> "It should be a delight to feel heat strike the skin, a delight to stand upright, knowing the bones are moving easily under the flesh."
> **Doris Lessing, contemporary novelist**

The more attentive and appreciative you are of the myriad of pleasurable, inspiring, and gratifying opportunities that surround you, the greater your joy, positive impact on others, ability to handle difficult situations, and capacity to recharge and rejuvenate.

You may express these celebrations with smiles, laughter, a victory dance, or prayer, but you may not. The expression of feelings may take place within, invisible to others, except perhaps for the subtle aura of joy and peace emitted by your bubbling spirit.

You don't have to be on an exotic vacation to become filled with awe at the sight of a sunset. Just take two minutes, any late afternoon, walk outside, look to the west, and open your eyes. You need not wait for a big-splurge dinner at a fancy restaurant to really enjoy a meal. You can relish every bite of food. Experience the sweetness, sourness, heat, and cold. Observe and enjoy as the taste lingers in your mouth. Be thankful for being blessed with such abundance.

> ## "Slow down and enjoy life."
> **Eddie Cantor, early twentieth-century
> star of stage and screen**

Even though small, private celebrations are enjoyable and important, at times, sharing feelings more publicly may enrich both you and others.

Hearing you play that song with such intensity and enthusiasm gives me goose bumps all over. I can really feel the music.

I must look like a fool with this big smile on my face, but I can't help it. Watching you so confidently and assertively deal with that man makes me feel very proud and happy.

*A great day at work, and then I come home and find you guys with your homework all done, helping your mom make a special dinner. Wow! It doesn't get any better than this.

Get started right away. Be on the lookout for any and all opportunities to celebrate. Grab hold and enjoy the ride.

> "Seize the moment. Remember all those women on the *Titanic* who waved off the dessert cart."
>
> **Erma Bombeck, humorist and author**

Examples of CELEBRATING

Following an emotional, exhausting, intense weekend preparing her state and federal tax returns, Joan jumped to her feet and joyously danced from room to room chanting, *Who the woman? I the woman! Who the woman? I the woman!* When she finished her victory dance, she rushed to her computer to announce to the world via Facebook that she had, with no help, completed her taxes and was going to receive modest state and federal refunds.

> "Love the moment, and the energy of that moment will spread beyond all boundaries."
> **Sister Corita Kent, nun, teacher, and religious artist**

After years of bouncing from diet to diet, sixty-seven-year-old Carol hoped and prayed this would be the program that worked for her. As she walked toward the scale, her mind raced. *I've followed the rules 100 percent for seven days now. I just know it's working. I can feel it.* Apprehension washed across her face as she peered over her round midsection and looked down at the scale. She stepped off, breathed deeply, and thought, *It's only two pounds, but at least I'm going in the right direction. Way to go, me! I think the time is right for a celebratory speed-walk around the neighborhood.*

A massive heart attack opened Rick's eyes to a new world.

I'm sixty-three, but I feel like my life is just beginning. Today was my first full day home from the hospital. When I woke up this morning and heard the wind blowing through the tree branches, I couldn't help but smile, and I started singing. I feel so alive and free and connected to everything and everyone around me. When I shaved, the warm water on my face and the tingle of the shaving cream reminded me of what a great gift it is to feel. I'm through taking life for granted. The new me is going to appreciate every taste, every sight, and every sound.

"Stop worrying about the potholes in the road and celebrate the journey."
Barbara Hoffman, JD, cancer survivor and author

Review

Celebrate both **large** and **small events, the process** as well as **the product**, either **privately, publicly, or both**.

❁

Self-Reflection

Look back over your past twenty-four hours and recall when, why, and how you engaged in any type of *celebration*.

CHAPTER 6

NEGOTIATE AGREEMENTS THROUGH COMPROMISE

....

"You cannot shake hands with a clenched fist."
Indira Gandhi, first woman prime minister of
India (1966–1977 and 1980–1984)

....

Why is NEGOTIATING important?

There's no published road map for your life. It's up to you to negotiate where you're going and how you'll get there. You negotiate with yourself to determine how you'll expend your energy, and you negotiate with others to establish guidelines and boundaries for your relationships. The more consciously you engage in this process, the better the fit between your values and choices and between yourself and others.

Putting ample thought and care into negotiating with yourself magnifies the likelihood your days will be spent working toward goals that will benefit you the most.

It took a lot of thought and soul-searching before I decided to leave my safe though unfulfilling and boring job and go off on my own, but it has worked out great—I love running my own business and being in charge of my destiny.

Putting ample thought and care into negotiating with others leads to stronger, more committed partnerships.

Our deal was he'd put in one-third of the start-up costs, and my share would be two-thirds, but he'd be the full-time, on-site, managing owner, and I'd only come in two and a half days a week and be in charge of handling accounting and contracts.

What is more, negotiation can give you increased motivation to strive for success.

I'm working so hard because my wife and I made a deal: she'd support us for two years while I work on marketing the inventions I've developed over the past decade.

> "Every human benefit and enjoyment, every virtue and every prudent act, is founded on compromise and barter."
>
> **Edmund Burke, eighteenth-century British statesman and author**

How to NEGOTIATE

Prior to any negotiation, within yourself or between yourself and others, you must first and foremost separate needs from wants and achievable goals from impossible dreams.

Needs are the nonnegotiable, absolute, minimal requirements your life demands; wants are negotiable, flexible, desirable preferences you could exist without.

*I need a minimum of seven hours of sleep each night. I want eight or nine hours.

*I need to earn $70,000 a year to cover expenses. I want to earn $500,000 a year.

Which of your dreams are achievable, and which aren't? Achievable dreams are worth planning and working toward; they deserve your attention and efforts.

*If I set my mind to it, I really could handle a couple of years of night school and finally finish that MBA program I dropped out of years ago.

For years I've dreamed about taking a year off and sailing around the Caribbean. If this year goes as well as last, I just might be able to make it happen.

Impossible dreams need to be recognized as such and discarded or altered.

I need to let go of the fantasy that I'll be the first high school dropout elected president of the United States. But I might someday earn a seat on the city council or maybe even be mayor.

Considering I just turned fifty, I guess my dream of being a professional football player is never going to come true. But I could volunteer to help coach the local high school team.

Who are you? What do you value? What's negotiable, and what isn't? What's achievable, and what isn't? Negotiation, based on a strong sense of self and a solid grounding in reality, ensures that the results of negotiation will be assimilated more compatibly into your being.

After needs are separated from wants and achievable dreams are distinguished from impossible dreams, you can enter into negotiations with an open mind. This is best done through a three-stage process, a process that can take place within yourself as you make personal decisions or when negotiating with others.

> "The ingenious human capacity for maneuver and compromise may make acceptable tomorrow what seems outrageous or impossible today."
>
> **William V. Shannon, twentieth-century American newspaperman and editor**

The first step in negotiation is to make a list of all possible options. Sometimes referred to as *brainstorming*, this process usually works best when ideas are allowed to flow freely, and many possible choices are generated before any analysis takes place. Evaluating each idea as it comes up slows and often blocks the creative process. The goal here is to open yourself to as many possibilities as possible. Far too many of us, far too often, decide far too quickly on ideas that won't work and courses of action that can't be achieved.

Once a list (ideally, a written list) of possibilities is generated, the next step is to honestly and openly consider each one. Eliminate ideas that all parties agree are undesirable, and make an effort to merge options that are similar.

It seems to me we're agreed that divorce, separation, and sleeping in separate rooms are not options we want to consider. That leaves us with three ideas: setting up a daily time to communicate without any distractions, marriage counseling, and individual counseling, so let's talk about these options...

> "If you want to make peace with your enemy,
> you have to work with your enemy.
> Then he becomes your partner."
> **Nelson Mandela, long-imprisoned political activist
> and first black president of South Africa**

Finally, it's usually best to agree on easier aspects of the negotiation before tackling more difficult ones. This creates a positive rhythm or mind-set. *This can be done. Progress is being made.* It establishes a momentum or positive flow in the negotiation and sets up all participants as winners.

> *So it's agreed. We're going to have at least ten minutes of uninterrupted time to communicate, every night, right after dinner, and we're going to enter some form of counseling, together or separately, which we'll start before the first of the month.*

All parties in a negotiation need to feel like winners; they need to feel their most essential needs are being met. If this doesn't occur, if the negotiation leads to one party "winning" and the other party "losing," the relationship suffers, and there's a good chance the "loser" will see to it that the "winner" doesn't really get what he or she expected.

Examples of NEGOTIATING

Fifty-two-year-old Lily explains that because she was sure about what she wanted, negotiations were successful.

I used to hate my job. I saw the nurses working with patients and doing all this life-saving, important stuff, and I was just cleaning up after them. After three years of that, I became really focused on my desire to become a nurse. I should have shared more of my frustrations and dreams with my husband sooner, but at least I knew what I wanted before we started discussing it. I didn't let my husband's skepticism, our limited funds, my unsupportive parents, or the fact that we had two kids in middle school stop me. We worked out a plan, and now here I am, a registered nurse, and loving it.

Bonnie, a retired postal-service employee, opened a catering business with her out-of-work daughter.

The two of us were just about ready to close up shop, to shut down the business because of constant disagreements about who was responsible for what, our long-range plans, and a number of other friction points. As a last resort, we went for counseling. Our counselor was incredible. She made us start with the easier issues and work on one thing at a time: focus on one issue; agree on how we wanted it to be; come up with possible solutions; pick one; do it; evaluate our progress. First, we agreed on job descriptions for each of us, then a system to monitor our preparedness for each job, and most recently, a set meeting time each week to look at the big picture of our schedules, months in advance. Working together is so much better since we started negotiating through these details. The key is starting with the easier issues and letting your successes pave the way for the harder ones.

> "It still holds true that man is most uniquely human when he turns obstacles into opportunities."
>
> **Eric Hoffer, twentieth-century American political and social philosopher and author**

James, a tall, thin, balding plumber, boasts about the success of an important compromise.

Ever since I turned eighteen, Sundays were for drinking beer and watching sports with my buddies. Until the divorce, I never realized this was a problem for my first wife. Then I was single for a few years and continued spending every Sunday with my buddies. But when Rosa and I started talking about getting married, she told me, "I'm not going to sit home every Sunday while you and 'the boys' do your thing. Sundays have to be for church and family." We talked and talked and finally agreed I could have every other Sunday afternoon with friends, but every Sunday morning and every other Sunday afternoon was for us and the kids. (We both have grown kids and grandkids.) Well, we've been married seven years, and it's going great. If we hadn't been a little flexible, we would have lost each other.

"Lasting change is a series of compromises.
And compromise is all right, as long as your
values don't change."

**Jane Goodall, English zoologist who works to protect
the habitats of chimpanzees**

Review

Negotiate from an **understanding of personal needs
and wants** and **achievable versus impossible
dreams** by being **open to all possible solutions**
and **finding common ground** before trying to solve
difficult issues.

❈

Self-Reflection

Put yourself in the place of the person you care most
about and contemplate how he or she would describe
your *negotiating* style?

CHAPTER 7

INFLUENCE YOURSELF AND OTHERS IN POSITIVE DIRECTIONS

"You are what you think about all day long."
Robert Schuller, television minister and author

Why is INFLUENCING important?

Every thought, every word from your lips, every action you take influences who you are, your immediate environment, and to a lesser degree, the world at large. Imagine if every person you interacted with consistently looked upon, spoke of, and treated others poorly. At the opposite extreme, envision how different your daily existence might be if people looked upon, spoke of, and treated each other with respect. Small actions add up.

You have a choice: consciously work on self-improvement, on becoming more loving, caring, and accomplished; or accept that who you are, how you think, speak, and act is not under your control. You can let life happen or take charge.

Besides influencing yourself, your words and actions influence those closest to you: relatives, friends, and co-workers. You can choose to be a role model and have a positive effect on their lives, or you can ignore this opportunity and have a lesser, or perhaps even negative, impact.

> "To be alive is to be powerful.
> Every time we think, feel, or act, we exert power and influence the world."
> **Gloria D. Karpinski, holistic counselor, spiritual director, and author**

How to INFLUENCE

You may not be a professional athlete, high-profile elected official, or movie star; however, how you think, speak, and behave influences not only who you are and who you are becoming but others as well. The choice isn't to influence versus not to influence. The choice is the direction of your influence.

I find the more I smile at people, the more they smile back; the more I treat them with respect, the more they treat me with respect; and the more I give, the more I receive.

The reason I drive a gas-efficient car, recycle, and conserve energy in my home is because I'm concerned about the environment. I can't tell others how to live their lives, but I can live a life consistent with my beliefs.

The influence of others is often like a strong current, one that can help move you more quickly and directly on your intended path. Conversely, the influence of others can also pull you in an unwanted direction. Pick friends, associates, and work environments carefully.

*If you wish to become more fit and athletic, you'll probably find the influence of a bicycling club more beneficial than that of a gourmet baking group.

*If you want to make progress toward a goal of occasional, limited, social drinking, you should spend less time in bars surrounded by heavy drinkers, and more time around individuals who rely less on alcohol.

"Keep five yards from a carriage, ten yards from a horse, and a hundred yards from an elephant; but the distance one should keep from a wicked man cannot be measured."
Indian Proverb

As others have the power to influence you, you have the power to influence others. This is true in all interactions, but your influence is most critical in regards to those closest to you.

*If you love playing an instrument or singing, your commitment to the development of these skills may significantly and positively encourage and influence your children, grandchildren, and those who love and hold you in esteem. Witnessing your focus, delight, and dedication provides them with a positive model.

*Taking an extra moment to enjoy a meal, to delight in the tastes and smells, and to appreciate what you have, may prompt those around you to do the same.

"Abundance is not something we acquire. It is something we tune into."
Wayne Dyer, self-help author, psychologist, and motivational speaker

Monitor the thoughts flowing through your consciousness, take charge of daydreams and fantasies, and direct your attention toward the achievement of your personal values and goals. Stop and reflect on your thoughts, and influence yourself to think more like the person you wish to become.

*I strive to be faithful and true to my wife. Fantasizing over the sexy redhead who works down the hall is taking me a giant step away from my intended destination. I'm going to erase these thoughts and replace them with something more positive and uplifting.

*When I'm playing tennis and hit the ball out, I get mad and critical of my abilities. I need to stop that *and remember I'm playing for fun, relaxation, and conditioning. I need to focus more on the smoothness and grace of my strokes and the joy I feel when I connect with the ball and less on the outcome.*

Every thought that flows through your mind, every word that crosses your lips, and every action you take influence who you are becoming. Your job is to design the self you want to be and bring that self to light.

"Only I can change my life. No one can do it for me."
Carol Burnett, comedian, singer, and television/movie star

Examples of INFLUENCING

Carlos, a successful financial consultant, started a local chapter of Big Brothers five years ago.

If it hadn't been for Big Brothers, I don't know what would have happened to me. My big brother, Ken, really saved me. He helped me see there was more in life than getting high and making it into a gang. He took me to concerts, sporting events, and lots of other stuff I had never experienced, and he helped me get through high school and formulate positive life goals. Now I'm a college graduate, with a great wife, kids, house, and life. I want to influence kids the way Ken influenced me. I want to make a difference.

> "The persuasion of a friend is a strong thing."
> **Homer, ancient Greek poet who composed the** *Iliad*
> **and the** *Odyssey*

Leo is clear and focused in his desire to improve his technology skills.

A few months ago, I applied for a promotion in my company. When I didn't get the job, I asked the personnel director what I could do to improve my chances the next time there was an opening. "Technology. It's all about technology," he replied. I said to myself, "I'm fifty-three-years old, smart, and want to get ahead. I can do tech if that's what they want." I enrolled in a programming class recommended by my supervisor, joined a couple of online, tech-oriented chat groups, and started eating lunch at the table where the techie group hangs out. They're all into the latest equipment and applications, and just being around them is like sitting in a graduate school seminar. If technology is what I need to get ahead, then I'm going to surround myself with it.

> "Example is not the main thing in influencing others. It is the only thing."
> **Dr. Albert Schweitzer, German born physician,**
> **medical missionary, theologian, and philosopher**

With great pride, Courtney states how her behavior positively influenced her daughter.

My daughter never studied much and always got terrible grades, until recently. This summer, I started working part-time on a graduate degree. Every second I can, I'm studying. The funny thing is, my daughter's grades have shot up. I guess she figured if her mom, a fifty-two-year-old single mother of two who works full-time, could study every night and get good grades, she could, too. I think my being in school and working so hard is really having a good influence on her.

Review

Influence yourself to **think, speak, and act consistently with who you are striving to become** and **influence others by the example you set.**

✺

Self-Reflection

Recall moments in the past twenty-four hours when you thought, said, or did something that was inconsistent with the person you strive to become.

CHAPTER 8

AIM FOR GOALS AND OBJECTIVES

"The person who makes a success of living is
the one who sees his goal steadily and
aims for it unswervingly."
Cecil B. DeMille, film director, producer, and writer

Why is AIMING important?

One of many magnificent opportunities life offers is the
chance to make dreams come true. You have a choice:
design and pursue the self you envision, or sit back and
watch as years float by and your unrealized potential lies
dormant. Designing the self you envision means deciding
who you want to be, aiming at long-term goals, setting

short-term objectives to help you get there, and working diligently toward their achievement. These choices profoundly affect who you will be tomorrow and for the rest of your life.

I almost stopped studying Spanish when our son was born. I'm so glad I didn't. I always dreamed I'd some-day be bilingual, and now I am.

We were like clones of one another when we were younger. Now you've got it all, and my life is a mess. What happened?

The answer to "What happened?" usually comes down to AIMING at your direction in life, rather than leaving it to chance. This isn't easy work. It involves thought, time, and commitment. But great rewards rarely just drop into your lap!

> "The first step to getting the things you want out of life is this: Decide what you want."
> **Ben Stein, writer and television personality**

How to AIM

The first step in aiming at goals and objectives is clarifying what you want. What are your likes and dislikes, values, needs, desires, and dreams? As you look within and determine the key components of who you are, questions will arise. *Why am I here? How strong are my values and beliefs? What do I want out of life?* The importance of this questioning process cannot be overemphasized! Too many individuals become involved in careers, relationships, lifestyles, and retirement plans without first determining whether they are good fits.

> *We picked this retirement community because we thought it would be a good match for us in our seventies and eighties, and we disregarded the fact that we're just in our early sixties. This place is making me CRAZY!*

> *We love living in the middle of a lot of action—live music, coffee houses, theater, and ethnic restaurants. Someday we might want a slower, quieter lifestyle, but for now, we are in just the right spot.*

There may be instances where two aspects of your personality conflict with one another. (*I love the peace and solitude of nature and the excitement and variety of city life.*) Or there may be times when your need is in conflict with that of a loved one. (*He wants a big couch, coffee table, chair, and TV in the room, but I love the Zen feeling of very little furniture.*) You may need to compromise, but you should do this with your eyes open, which requires that you know yourself.

Once you have a clear picture of your likes and dislikes, values, needs, desires, and dreams, and a sense of how strong or important each is to you, you're ready for the next step, creating a visual picture of who and what you might someday become. Focus on one specific area at a time, and imagine if you put in the time and energy, where might it take you? How far could you go with this in the next ten or twenty years?

I love ballroom dancing and want to learn as many forms as I can to the point where I can get out there for every song, not think about the steps, and just be in the flow and let my creativity take over. I picture myself at seventy-five, eighty, eighty-five years old still dancing and having a ball!

Money, nice things, and financial security, that's what I'm going for. When I stop working, I want to travel wherever I want and be able to take the kids and grandkids along for the ride without worrying about the expense.

Way up there on my list of priorities is helping and sharing my life with family and friends. On my eightieth birthday, I want to be surrounded by loved ones whose lives are intertwined with mine.

"It is not enough to understand what we ought to be, unless we know what we are; and we do not understand what we are, unless we know what we ought to be."
T.S. Eliot, American poet and 1948 recipient of the Nobel Prize for literature

When you have a picture of who you are and where you want to go, once your goals are set, it's time to devise shorter term, specific objectives to move in that direction, and then get to work achieving them.

*Long-term goal: *I love bluegrass and want to play guitar well enough to spontaneously and effortlessly join other musicians in jam sessions.*
Short-term objectives: *I need to find a teacher, buy a guitar, and formulate a regular practice schedule.*

*Long-term goal: *I want to learn sign language so I can communicate better with my great-niece, who's deaf.*
Short-term objectives: *I'm going to enroll in a class, buy some CDs and flashcards, and start studying fifteen minutes each night before bed.*

*Long-term goal: *I want to be more consistent and knowledgeable about my vegetarian diet and maybe eliminate eggs and dairy and go totally vegan.*
Short-term objectives: *It's time to start reading about nutrition and diet and get a garden going, maybe take an organic gardening class.*

"Go confidently in the direction of your dreams. Live the life you have imagined."
Henry David Thoreau, nineteenth-century American writer and philosopher

---

Like the Nike ad says, "Just do it." The best-laid plans are meaningless without follow-through. In order for your life to go in the direction of your dreams, take aim at important goals, and make a commitment to work on the short-term objectives that will lead you there.

Examples of AIMING

Ron usually feels fulfilled and satisfied managing the local supermarket. His wife, Karen, enjoys baking gourmet pies, which she sells to restaurants in the Denver area. But Ron and Karen share a dream.

After two years of talking and negotiating, Karen and I have decided we want to move closer to our son and his family in Santa Fe and open up a little bakery. In order to make that happen, we figure we'll need to get the house here ready to put up for sale; start cashing in some of our investments; research possible locations for the bakery; and start discussions with our son and daughter-in-law about how close or far away from them they'd like us to locate.

"It's crucial for a couple to have shared goals and values. The more you have in common the less you have to argue about."
Barbara Friedman, author and motivational speaker

At the age of sixty-four, Cindy focused on her goal of someday playing violin in the local symphony.

I've been playing violin on and off for the past fifty-five years. I was quite good in high school and college, but between raising four kids and helping my husband with his business, my skills have atrophied over the past forty years. Well, if my dream is ever going to come true, I need to get to work. My plan is to start taking lessons from a lady I know who's the concert master of our symphony, join a local string quartet, and practice, practice, practice.

> "I never see what has been done; I only see what remains to be done."
>
> **Madame Marie Curie, two-time Nobel Prize winner in science**

Bill hasn't talked to his daughter in fifteen years and has never met his five-year-old grandson.

As I look back over my life and into my future, I feel empty and alone. I messed up the most important relationships I could ever have. I'd trade everything to be part of my daughter's and grandson's lives. I mailed a letter today, apologizing for being such a louse all these years and pleading to let me into their lives. I'm going to telephone in a few days and ask to schedule a get-together. No matter how she responds, I'm not going to give up. Whether she agrees to see me or not, I'm going to start sending birthday cards and gifts from this day forward, and I'm going to keep trying, with letters and phone calls, to be a part of their family.

> "Don't be afraid of the space between your dreams and reality.
> If you can dream it, you can make it so."
> **Bette Davis, actress and Hollywood diva**

Review

Aim at **identifying likes and dislikes, values, needs, desires, and dreams** and **formulating long-term goals and short-term objectives** to achieve desired results.

❈

Self-Reflection

Consider one important goal you are *aiming* toward and recall what you have done this past week to work toward that goal?

CHAPTER 9

DARE TO ACT BOLDLY

"You get in life what you have the courage to ask for."
Oprah Winfrey, television personality, producer,
and philanthropist

Why is DARING important?

You can be what others expect you to be, fit in, and not make waves, or dare to be yourself. *I'm a grandmother and a skydiver. I don't care what my daughter says is or isn't appropriate.*

You can sit back and play it safe, expect and demand little from life, and insulate yourself from the anxiety that often accompanies striving for goals, or dare to push the boundaries of your comfort levels.

I'm nervous about taking the early retirement program my company is offering, but I'm really, really ready to try something different. My wife and I are always talking about someday living full-time in our summer cabin and opening up a little bed and breakfast. If not now, when?

You can allow others to make decisions for you, not take chances, and wait patiently for your future to unfold, or dare to act and risk failure. *If I ask him out, and he says no, I'll feel stupid, but he's too shy to ever ask me, so I'm going for it.*

Daring isn't easy. It often ends in setbacks and failures. But without it, your sense of self is diminished, and accomplishments are less than they might have been.

> "If we listened to our intellect, we'd never have a love affair.
> We'd never have a friendship. We'd never go into business...
> Well, that's nonsense.
> You've got to jump off cliffs all the time and build your wings on the way down."
> **Annie Dillard, contemporary essayist and fiction author**

How to DARE

Daring to be yourself requires self-understanding. Do you really want to quit your job and go backpacking around the world, or do you love your job and life and just need a few weeks off to unwind? Is she really the woman of your dreams, or is it her great looks and the ego-satisfaction you feel being seen with her that are bringing on these thoughts of marriage? Look within, question, listen, watch, check for consistency between your heart, thoughts, words, and actions, and evaluate what it all means. Introspection, reading, studying, meditation, psychotherapy, talking with friends...the paths to self-understanding are numerous.

The gains from daring to know yourself are important but don't lead very far without the next step—daring to be yourself and pushing the boundaries of your comfort level.

I just recently learned how to say no. Before, I let everyone lead me and push me around. I guess I was afraid of not being liked or accepted. It's still hard for me to say no, but when I do, it feels honest and right.

Moving into management hasn't worked out very well. My wife and kids are proud of me and love the money I'm bringing in and the new life we're able to afford, but I hate my job. I'm thinking about going back to working in the field, even though everyone will think I'm crazy if I do.

I absolutely love working in the flower shop. My husband and parents couldn't believe I'd turn my back on what had been a long and wonderful career as a dental hygienist, but I really wanted and needed the change.

> "You miss one hundred percent of the shots
> you never take."
> **Wayne Gretsky, National Hockey League Hall of
> Fame center known as the "Great One"**

As you expand your comfort level, stretch as much as you reasonably can. How far are you willing to go to get what you want? What will it take?

I'm sixty-two years old, tired all the time, and haven't exercised in years, but I want to run a marathon. Starting today, my first baby step toward my goal is to walk or walk-jog around the high school track every afternoon for at least one hour.

I want to get my novel published, but none of the agents or publishers I've written have given me one word of encouragement. I've decided to use some of my savings to self-publish and market the book myself.

> "Yesterday I dared to struggle.
> Today I dare to win."
> **Bernadette Devlin, elected to Parliament from
> Northern Ireland in 1969 at the age of twenty-one,
> the youngest-ever member of the British Parliament**

Following through on life-altering agendas is rarely easy. If you change, friction, a period of disequilibrium, uncertainty, frustrations, roadblocks, and possible failures may litter your path to success. The hundred-mile bicycle ride may be beyond your present level of ability and leave you moaning in agony, cramped from head to toe at the side of the road. Or you may still be waiting for your first client a month after opening the website of your well-thought-out and highly publicized life-coaching business. There's always a chance you may fail, but without the willingness to push forward, to face and overcome fears and setbacks, you certainly won't achieve your dreams.

> "The future belongs to those who believe in the beauty of their dreams."
> **Eleanor Roosevelt, author, philosopher, and wife of President Franklin D. Roosevelt**

The best way to add more daring into your life is to begin with one area you feel the strongest about and the most able to commit to. Clarify what you hope to gain and which boundaries you might have to push to get there, and then get to work. Daring is rarely easy but has the potential of truly great rewards.

Examples of DARING

Two years ago, Amanda, a fifty-nine-year-old third-grade teacher, considered retiring after twenty-eight years in the classroom.

I was burnt-out, sick and tired of being forced to brainlessly implement the dry, boring, uncreative, overly demanding curriculum my school district demanded. Fortunately, I decided to give teaching one more year, on my own terms. I took all the books and curriculum guides I was supposed to use, stuck them in the closet, and involved my students in planning units of instruction and lessons that were much more interesting and involving. I was still working on all the skills I was supposed to cover, but in a way that fit the students and me much better. Every few weeks I received written warnings from my principal, telling me I was in violation of district policies, but I didn't care. I felt I was doing the right thing. At the end of the year, my students scored incredibly well on the district and state tests, and other teachers nominated me for teacher of the year.

Looking back over his life, Raymond regrets spending most of it in the closet, hiding his homosexuality.

I was about eleven or twelve when I realized I was gay, but I spent the next fifty years hiding it from friends, my parents, my wife and children, and everyone else. For fifty years, I kept my secret and suffered tremendous guilt and self-loathing. When I turned sixty, I went into psychotherapy and realized I couldn't continue the lie any longer. It was hard, incredibly hard coming out to family, friends, and coworkers, admitting I was gay. My transition from guilt-ridden, unbalanced, confused, pretend-straight Raymond, to more confident, goal-directed, self-accepting, gay Raymond took over three years— three years of confusion, clarity, embarrassment, confidence, depression, and elation. It's been a long and hard process but definitely worth the effort.

> "Expect trouble as an inevitable part of life
> and when it comes, hold your head high, look
> it squarely in the eye and say,
> 'I will be bigger than you. You cannot defeat me.'"
> **Ann Landers, popular American
> newspaper advice columnist**

Jason, a single, successful, and financially secure fifty-year-old attorney, still cherishes a lifelong dream of joining the Peace Corps and working in Africa.

Everyone I know thinks I'm crazy. But I figure if I don't take any chances, I might just as well dig a hole, jump in, and bury myself. I'm not going to sit here in my little office for the rest of my life and forget about all the exciting things I want to do just because other people think I should do this or that. I've gathered all the information on the Peace Corps and a couple of other, similar volunteer organizations, and I am real close to signing up, if one of them will have me.

> "You may be disappointed if you fail, but you
> are doomed if you don't try."
> **Beverly Sills, opera singer and
> prolific charity fundraiser**

Review

Dare to be yourself, to push the boundaries of your comfort level, and to risk failure.

�֍

Self-Reflection

What secrets do you hold? What are the costs and benefits of holding onto them?

CHAPTER 10

UPGRADE EXPECTATIONS

"A successful individual typically sets
his next goal somewhat but not too
much above his last achievement.
In this way he steadily raises his level of aspiration."
Kurt Lewin, Gestalt psychologist and
cofounder of Group Dynamics

Why is UPGRADING important?

The answer to the age-old question, "Is that all there is?" is a resounding *no*! If you make the effort, there are and will always be more goals to strive for, love to feel and express, people to meet and grow close to, knowledge to gain, and experiences to appreciate at deeper and deeper levels. Expect and work toward more from and for yourself. Consider how improved your life is because your parents, grandparents, or great-grandparents left their birthplace in search of something better or because you moved on from your first, low-skill, low-wage job.

Consider how improved the world is because Mother Teresa left her position as a classroom teacher and founded the Missionaries of Charity or because Dwight D. Eisenhower continued working after great success as a field general and went on to lead the Allies to victory in World War II and finally serve as president of the United States.

Once you've achieved, or nearly achieved, a long-term goal, upgrading to a new, more challenging, or different target can be an energizing, rejuvenating experience that leads you further than you originally planned or dreamed.

> "The world is round and the place which may seem like the end may also be the beginning."
> **Ivy Baker Priest, secretary of the treasury under President Dwight D. Eisenhower**

How to UPGRADE

An important key to upgrading is remaining open to the process of continual improvement and the belief that the quality of your life and relationships can be better. This doesn't mean you have to strive constantly for something different or more; it means that you should consider the possibilities. You can fully appreciate what you have and at the same time look forward to and work for what is yet to come.

> "Ever since my first lesson, I've been impatient to learn more. I'm always saying, 'OK, I've learned [a particular skating skill]. What's next?' I still feel that way."
> **Michelle Kwan, nine-time US figure-skating champion and five-time world champion**

Perhaps your present residence is the biggest, most comfortable, most fabulous home you've ever lived in. Perhaps you don't need or want more. But if you do, be aware of your dreams and desires, and if their fulfillment is important, work toward them.

Perhaps your present residence is the biggest, most comfortable, most fabulous home you've ever lived in, but the cost (financial, physical, emotional...) of staying there is too great. Maybe an upgrade in quality of life and life-style (lower payments, less yard work, shorter commute, more time with family...) requires a downgrade in the size and expense of your home.

Many people believe professional and financial success requires them to live in a bigger home, drive a flashier car, and take more expensive vacations; however, it doesn't have to be that way! Upgrading as described here means upgrading the match or compatibility between how you spend the moments and hours in your life and what brings you joy, peace, and fulfillment. Most important is that the upgrade should raise your satisfaction with life and keep you moving toward fulfilling your potential.

Upgrading your appreciation of life requires a greater focus on the here and now. Slow down, purge thoughts that aren't relevant to the moment, and apply your senses and mind to immediate experiences. Believe that the walk you're about to take, the drive you're embarking on, and the salad on your plate will be equal to or better than the best you've ever had. Believe it, and make it so.

In every town and city in the world, there are many individuals who can afford only the most plain and basic foods, yet they appreciate the tastes and nourishment received from each meal far more than some who dine in the finest restaurants. There are people who never travel more than a few miles from where they dwell, yet delight in new and novel experiences more than some who lavishly trek the world seeking unique and different thrills. There are those who live joyously and peacefully in fulfilling, dynamic relationships with partners who are not physically beautiful, rich, famous, or powerful, but who give far more to and gain far more from their partners than some who are physically beautiful, rich, famous, or powerful.

Upgrading your appreciation of life means gaining more joy, satisfaction, and personal growth, regardless of the size boat you're traveling in, the exoticness of the vacation spot you've selected, or the price of the seat you're watching the game from.

"The more we see, the more we are
capable of seeing."
**Maria Mitchell, nineteenth-century astronomer and
president of the American Association for the
Advancement of Women**

Upgrading does not mean you need to formulate continuously more demanding, higher-level goals. Ideally, you will periodically review your goals and consider developing new ones; however, you don't have to spend your entire life working toward more, faster, longer, better.

*As your skills playing music advance, you may decide to upgrade to harder pieces, but you may decide instead to stay with the same music for a while and upgrade tone, creative expression, or ability to play from memory.

*Whereas you might decide to upgrade your ten-kilometer run expectations from fifty minutes to forty-five minutes, you might seek a different type of upgrade, like running the next race with a constant focus on your breath and surroundings.

*When the time approaches for the purchase of your next car, you may decide to upgrade to a more expensive or prestigious model; however, your upgrade may be to a more fun, economical, or dependable ride.

There are sunsets, clouds, and vistas as or more beautiful than you've ever seen before, and there are opportunities to love as or more deeply than you've ever achieved. All are out there, waiting. Your job is to expect, search for, find, and appreciate them.

> "In some ways, spiritual growth resembles a game of leapfrog."
> **Jean Grasso Fitzpatrick, contemporary American author and psychologist**

Examples of UPGRADING

Luke, a fifty-six-year-old security guard, has been living with his girlfriend, April, for six years.

> *We used to play all sorts of sports together, go to movies and museums, and keep so busy there never seemed to be enough hours in the day. Then, a few weeks ago, we realized all we ever did was sit around eating and watching TV. We're turning into the half-dead-inside fifty-somethings we swore we'd never become. Then and there we made a pledge to keep more on top of our relationship. We had just assumed our life together would get better and better, and we hadn't realized we needed to keep working on it.*

"I can't imagine going on when there are no more expectations."

Dame Edith Evans, British stage and screen actress

Although it was almost fifty years ago, Eleanor remembers herself as a twenty-year-old culinary school student in Paris.

> *Each day was a new world of experiences. I had everything one could wish for, including a deep, abiding appreciation for my good fortune. Little did I know I was just scratching the surface of who I could be. As the decades passed, my life got better and better. This wasn't by accident. Over the years I traveled extensively, met and spent time with a continuous stream of amazing people, taught and took many college courses, did in-depth reading and research in various*

areas, and worked diligently to continue growing as a person, chef, wife, mother, and human being.

Eli, a successful journalist at a prestigious newspaper, fell into an extended funk a number of years ago after being awarded a Pulitzer Prize for a series of articles he had researched and written.

I was forty-nine years old at the time, and I had achieved everything I had dedicated myself to for the past twenty years. I should have been happy and content, but I felt empty and directionless. My problem was I had reached all my professional goals, and I hadn't formed any new ones. It took me a few weeks to figure out why I felt so empty, but once I did, I went right into action, planning out a book I dreamed of writing. The process of getting started on the book brought me back to life.

"All our dreams can come true—if we have the courage to pursue them."

Walt Disney, creator of Mickey Mouse and founder of Walt Disney Enterprises

Review

Be open to opportunities to **upgrade your appreciation of life, personal goals**, and the **quality of your relationships**.

✻

Self-Reflection

Fill in the blanks: I am most interested in *upgrading* the quality of my relationship with _____. What I'd like to achieve in this relationship is _____. Steps I'm thinking of taking to achieve this are _____.

CHAPTER 11

START TO DO WHAT NEEDS TO BE DONE

"It's a job that's never started that takes
the longest to finish."
J. R. R. Tolkien, twentieth-century British scholar
and author of *The Lord of the Rings* and *The Hobbit*

If you don't start, you'll never finish.

Thinking, analyzing, and planning are good, but lead nowhere without accompanying action. To get things done, you need to do, move, engage.

How many times have you had a great idea that you never followed up on? The idea, without the follow-up, has no life or form. How often have you questioned your ability to accomplish something yet taken the first step anyway and found each succeeding step easier and easier as you grew closer to reaching your goal? To accomplish distant, long-term goals, you must first work on more immediately achievable, short-term objectives.

If you feel like you can't get out of bed, and you lie there, minute after minute, hour after hour, motionless, contemplating all you have to do, the day isn't going to be very productive. If you feel like you can't get out of bed, but you make an effort to throw off the covers, you're soon on your feet, ready to turn possibilities into probabilities and probabilities into realities.

Why start? Because you probably want more of something: more connectedness, skills, experiences, money, free time...And having or getting more requires action.

> "My future starts when I wake up every morning... Every day I find something creative to do with my life."
>
> **Miles Davis, influential American jazz trumpeter and bandleader**

How to START

Once you have devoted sufficient thought, analysis, and planning to your goal, it's time to start doing.

This begs the question of what sufficient means in this context. Sufficient here implies that the following three issues have been addressed:

1. **Is your goal or objective clear?** You don't want to start, to invest too much of yourself, unless you've

looked far enough ahead to feel fairly confident this is the direction you want to go.

- If you want to start getting in shape, first decide if your primary goal is to lose a few pounds, gain strength, or prepare for involvement in a specific sport. Where are you going?
- Do you want to start learning more about wine because you want to enjoy it more, increase your wine cellar, or qualify for the new opening of wine steward at the upscale restaurant where you work? Why do you want to study wines?

2. **Do you have the time, money, health, and motivation to make a good effort?** If not, perhaps you should prepare a bit more before starting.
   - You probably shouldn't start the car trip if you don't have enough gas money to reach and return from your destination.
   - Starting to plan a wedding may be the right thing to do if you're in love and ready to settle down and make a long-term commitment.
   - Do you really want to follow through on the plans you made years ago with an old friend to someday spend a month trekking in the Himalayas? Is the motivation still there? Is your body still capable?

3. **How great a risk factor can you handle?** Some people aren't ready to start until every detail has been planned for, every obstacle considered, and every option analyzed. Others require and desire far less organization and certainty.
   - *I want to liquidate all my investments so I can take advantage of the stock tip my brother gave me, but I'm scared. Maybe I should put only half or a quarter of what I have into this.*

- *We've put a lot of effort into researching how to get the most money from the sale of our house. And we've put the same effort into studying the real estate market where we plan on moving. We're a little nervous about the move but confident that we have all the information we need.*

"You sort of start thinking anything's possible if you've got enough nerve."
J. K. Rowling, contemporary British author of the
Harry Potter **series**

Once the goal or objective is clear, resources are sufficient, and you're able to live with the risks inherent in what you're about to begin, it's time to plan out a sequence of steps to move in that direction.

It's often difficult to take the first step. Many people never start because they're uncertain of the outcome, concerned they won't succeed, or unable to summon the energy and drive to move through all that must be done. When this is the case, begin small and start with something easy.

I may or may not actually go to the gym and work out, but I'm going to put on my shorts and sneakers. It's possible that merely putting on my exercise clothes will be all the start I need to move to the next step.

I'm not ready to promise myself I'll finish all I'd have to do to get my broker's license, but I can commit to attending the introductory meeting on what the process would entail.

I'd like to get rid of all the junk in the basement and reorganize the stuff that's worth keeping, but my goal today is just to get started by hauling all the old magazines and newspapers to the recycle bin. Even though the old magazines and newspapers are only a small part of the job, at least they're a beginning.

Start by selecting an easy-to-accomplish, less threatening or intimidating part of the total job you hope to tackle, and begin there. Success most often leads to increased motivation and further successes.

Examples of STARTING

Leanne, a sixty-year-old police dispatcher, rekindled an old love.

I did one little project with clay sculpting in high school and fell in love with it. Ever since then, the idea of working with clay popped into my head every now and again. Two years ago, I made up my mind that I couldn't wait any longer. I went to the craft store and spent fifty dollars on clay and assorted tools and set up an area in the garage. A few weeks later I signed up for an evening class at the local high school. Before long, I was spending two or three hour-long sessions a week in my garage, working in clay. Recently, I became involved with a group of sculptors who get together every weekend, and I love it. Sometimes I regret waiting so long, but mostly I'm happy I eventually did start and have this wonderful new activity in my life.

> "There is always another chance for you...you may have a fresh start any moment you choose..."
> **Mary Pickford, star of silent motion pictures, known as "America's Sweetheart"**

Felipe admits he should have faced his financial future sooner.

I can hardly believe we waited so long before starting to save for retirement. For years after we were married, there was barely enough money to get by, so we couldn't justify putting anything into accounts we wouldn't touch for decades. When we turned forty-five, my wife and I decided it was something that had to be done. Just opening the accounts was a huge step. For the past few years, we've been putting at least 10 percent of our gross income into them. We haven't gone without anything, but the accounts keep growing and growing. It was just getting started that was hard. The saving part is easy.

> "We must not...ignore the small differences we can make which, over time, add up to big differences..."
> **Marian Wright Edelman, author, social agitator, and founder of the** *Children's Defense Fund*

Sarah, a sixty-five-year-old retail clerk, used to have difficulty getting going Saturday mornings.

Every Saturday, I have a long list of jobs that have to be done. I used to waste a lot of time just sitting around, not really knowing where to start. Then I figured out the important thing was to just get going. All I need is to begin one job, then I'm rolling along and just barrel through all of them. What gets me going could be as simple as emptying the dishwasher or pulling the laundry hamper into the hallway. I pick something, anything that's quick and easy, and begin with that.

"The greatest step is out the door."
German Proverb

Review

Start with small, easily accomplished actions, after **you devote sufficient thought, analysis, and planning.**

❋

Self-Reflection

Think of one project you want to *start*, but haven't, and a first step you might take to get it going.

CHAPTER 12

WORK WITH A POSITIVE ATTITUDE AND PASSION

"Far and away the best prize that life offers is the chance to work hard at work worth doing."
Theodore Roosevelt, twenty-sixth president of the United States

Why is WORKING important?

It is through work that human beings expand their sense of personal identity and purpose, combine knowledge, skills, and efforts in order to contribute to one another, and support themselves and their families.

Whether your work is volunteering in a homeless shelter, cutting hair, building shopping centers, designing jewelry, or providing childcare, it has a purpose. Someone is served through your efforts.

The primary motivating factor pushing most of us out the door and into the world of work is financial. We want that paycheck to support our lifelong habits of eating, sleeping indoors, paying for purchases, and contributing to retirement accounts. For others, the motivation is not financial but a need to contribute to society or a drive to express creativity or a desire to remain active and involved.

Whereas work is the most time-consuming activity the majority of humans participate in, it presents an excellent opportunity to develop skills, explore areas of potential, and achieve excellence.

> "You've achieved success in your field
> when you don't know whether what you're
> doing is work or play."
> **Warren Beatty, motion-picture actor, director,
> and producer**

How to WORK

You want a good match between who you are, your skills, lifestyle, preferences, and desires, and the work you do. Some enjoy working with people, whereas others choose less social interaction. Many people prefer a standard eight-to-five schedule; however there are those who would rather work night shifts. A little extra money and an opportunity to vary your schedule may be all you're looking for, but someone else's motivation may be a desire to contribute.

Earning a graduate degree or lucrative position as an engineer, accountant, or consultant is not a guarantee of job satisfaction and happiness, nor is the lack of a degree or a position in yard maintenance, delivering food to the elderly, or factory work a sentence to a life of dissatisfaction and disappointment.

Most critical is a good match between the demands and rewards of the work and your strengths and needs.

> "If you want to live in harmony with yourself, you have to work."
> **Maria Callas, one of the world's best-known sopranos of the mid-twentieth century**

Regardless of your age, learning more about job, career, or volunteer options is a good idea. The typical American, prior to retirement, will work in more than one career area and hold many different positions. For most, the days of working for thirty or forty years in the same job are gone. Therefore, it's never too late to investigate choices and plan ahead.

Whether you work for little money or a huge paycheck, from a desire to help others or help yourself, or in a prestigious or unglamorous position, you want to have a passion for what you do and a desire to do it well. That passion and desire can transform what might appear boring and mundane into something that is energizing and exciting.

*The bank teller who gains satisfaction from providing service to customers is probably well placed in his job.

*The bank manager who hates dealing with personnel issues may wish to consider moving to another position or career.

If you find it hard to enjoy, appreciate, and grow in the work you do, push yourself to look for the positive, or try to change job responsibilities, or enter personal or career counseling. Do whatever it takes to get to the place where work contributes to your wholeness, balance, and appreciation of life.

If your efforts to change your attitude toward your current work don't succeed, consider moving onto something different. Do you want to spend twenty or forty or sixty hours a week doing something you don't like? No. Does volunteering at a school when you can't stand being around kids make sense? No. Even if the money and benefits are great or the prestige or social importance is significant, a poor match between the work's responsibilities and your strengths and desires will almost certainly diminish your attitude, effectiveness, and both your mental and physical health.

Often, the decision to change a work situation is difficult, but there's almost always a way. Perhaps a move to a slightly different position is all that's required; or cutting back a few hours a week; or moving to a similar job, but in a different organization. A variety of solutions is usually possible.

Many look forward to their eventual departure from the world of work, expecting to live out their lives moving from one self-indulgent activity to the next: sleeping in, playing leisurely rounds of golf, lunching by the pool, afternoons playing cards, and so on. Unfortunately, this "all play and no work" lifestyle doesn't work well for everyone. After a few months, some retirees begin to crave a return to work, some way to use their skills, talents, and energy to contribute to others, perform a function, or make something.

It's good to plan and save for a retirement that does not require you to work in order to survive, but it's even better to do this while reserving some knowledge, skills, and energy so you can experience the joy and fulfillment of sharing your expertise with others.

> "All work done mindfully rounds us out, helps complete us as persons."
> **Marsha Sinetar, self-help/spirituality author, keynote speaker, and corporate advisor**

Examples of WORKING

Hank, a cabinetmaker, confidently defends his prices.

When clients tell me my bid is too high, I remind them, "You get what you pay for." Everything I do is custom, and I devote myself to it totally until it's finished. I don't rush through jobs, trying to squeeze the biggest possible profit out of them. As a matter of fact, I get so into my work I often lose track of time. Most of my clients wouldn't know the difference if I took a shortcut here or there, but I would. I make really good money doing what I love, but I don't do it just for the money. I do it because I enjoy working with wood and creating beautiful pieces of functional art.

> "Work for something because it is good, not just because it stands a chance to succeed."
> **Vaclav Havel, internationally renowned playwright and Czechoslovakia's first non-Communist president since 1948**

William, a fifty-four-year-old air force colonel, didn't last long as a retiree.

I had always planned to kick back, sleep late, and play a lot of golf and tennis after I retired. Well, that lasted about a year. I felt useless and unimportant, started having little squabbles with my wife, and helplessly observed as my cocktail hour moved from 5:00 p.m., to 3:00 p.m., to noon. So I rekindled an old dream of teaching high school social studies. I went back to school and in twelve months earned a secondary teaching credential. Now I teach world history and geography. I love teaching, am getting along much better with my wife, limit cocktail hours to an occasional TGIF or special event, and plan on working as long as they'll let me.

> ## "Laziness may appear attractive, but work gives satisfaction."
> **Lucille Ball, popular television comedian and star of the 1950s show** *I Love Lucy*

Sixty-two-year-old Barbara has served as an executive secretary in the same company for twenty-five years.

I had the same boss for the first nineteen years, and we got along great. When he retired, I began working for "the witch." Nothing was ever right or good enough for her. I started having stomach problems, didn't sleep well, and hated my job. Here's the worst part. I worked for her for four years *before applying for a transfer. Well, I'm still in the same company but have been in a different department with a fantastic boss for almost two years now. Once again, I feel appreciated, successful, and love being a secretary.*

"Work is love made visible.
And if you cannot work with love but only with distaste,
It is better that you should leave your work and
Sit at the gate of the temple and take alms of those who work with joy.
For if you bake bread with indifference,
You bake a bitter bread that feeds but half man's hunger."

Kahlil Gibran, early twentieth-century Lebanese painter and author of *The Prophet*

Review

Work with a **positive attitude and passion** for what you do, at **jobs that fit your personal profile**.

✺

Self-Reflection

Paid or unpaid, part- or full-time, consider the *work* you do and which aspects of it you feel the most passion for, the most wonderful connection with.

CHAPTER 13

FEEL EMOTIONS WITH BODY AND MIND

"I pay no attention whatever to anybody's
praise or blame.
I simply follow my own feelings."
Wolfgang Amadeus Mozart, eighteenth-century
Austrian composer

Why is FEELING important?

Love. Hate. Joy. Sadness. Peace. Anger. Feelings breathe
life into existence.

Adjusting your daughter's veil in preparation to walk
down the aisle; gazing upon a painting by Van Gogh; or

attending the funeral of a loved one are merely data-gathering ventures when void of feeling.

Experiencing and learning from the sensory responses associated with different emotions—changes in heart rate, blood pressure, breathing, muscle tension—that is, listening to your body, can help you be more in tune with emotions. *The second my boss walked into the room, I felt hot with anger, and my eyelids started twitching, which reminded me I needed to put in more time searching for a new job.*

By paying attention to your emotional responses and accompanying physical reactions—by feeling—you can better make choices in life that nurture both your mental and physical health.

> "I think one's feelings...
> ought all to be distilled into actions and into
> actions which bring results."
> **Florence Nightingale, British founder of the nursing
> profession as it is known today**

How to FEEL

First and foremost, experience feelings; don't ignore, block, or speed through them. Give yourself permission to feel. Stop, focus, and take a moment to remove emotional barriers, diversions, and rationalizations, and bring to the surface what's going on inside.

*Holding my newborn granddaughter makes me feel joyous. Colors appear brighter, my body feels so light I could float away, and a gentle tingle covers every inch of my skin.

*How dare he whip in front of me and take the parking space I've been waiting for. My heart is beating fast. I'm taking rapid, shallow breaths, and my head is hot and throbbing.

*I didn't get the promotion. I feel lethargic and heavy. Sights and sounds are dimmed and muffled. And my chest feels like an elephant stepped on it.

> "It is only with the heart that one can see rightly; what is essential is invisible to the eye."
> **Antoine de Saint-Exupery, pilot, poet, and author of**
> *The Little Prince*

Identify the feeling as it works its way around, through, and into your being. Notice how your body and mind are affected. Momentarily allow yourself to witness, without intervening.

Slow down and taste the anger, touch the excitement, and listen to the peace. This process can be profoundly revealing, rejuvenating, and life-enhancing, and it doesn't require much time. The human tendency to speed forward toward the fulfillment of objectives often makes the experiencing of feelings difficult.

*I don't have time to feel or express my anger—I need to get through this meeting and back to the office.

*Watching the sun set over the sea is so incredibly soothing and calming. Oh well, I don't want to waste *my whole afternoon with beauty and peace. I'd better get back on the road.*

"Better to be without logic than without feeling."
Charlotte Bronte, nineteenth-century British author

How long should you hold on to a feeling before moving on? Most psychologically healthy individuals tend to hold positive feelings a lot longer than negative ones.

*Holding onto a positive feeling: *My present blissful state of self-respect and optimism is interfering with my ability to finish this letter. To heck with the letter! It can wait five minutes.*

*Letting go of a negative feeling: *I'm so angry with him I can't think about anything else! But holding on to these feelings isn't going to improve the situation or get this tax return done. I'm going to take a deep, cleansing breath and let the anger go so I can get back to work.*

Once you've allowed yourself to fully experience an emotion, capture it in your memory. Then you can move onto evaluating what might have caused the feeling to emerge. How and why did you respond as you did? Do you want to repeat this cause-effect pattern in the future, or avoid it?

*Paul realized discussing politics with his uncle always led to intense and uncomfortable feelings of anger and resentment. He decided in the future he would change the subject when it came up, or if that weren't possible, he would simply walk away.

*Linda felt a warm, wonderful expansiveness through-out her body and a surge of optimism and energy after leading her first tour as a museum docent. By bringing awareness to her physical and emotional responses, she realized leading tours was right for her and decided to volunteer more regularly.

Resist the temptation to begin the analysis process until you've first had the opportunity to really experience the feeling. If you jump too quickly to mental processes, you may lose the feeling and not be able to regain it. There's a fine balance here. You don't want feeling without some analysis, nor do you want analysis based on insufficient, partial feeling.

Examples of FEELING

Tran, a part-time interpreter in his late sixties, excitedly shares his experience.

I've been blessed with the gift of feeling. Many times a day, every cell in my body is filled with emotion. Most often the emotion is a positive one, like love, honor, or awe, but sometimes I do experience fear, anxiety, impatience, and all the rest. One technique I've developed over the years is experiencing the feeling and then letting it go. I acknowledge the feeling and let it fill me up, and then I analyze what's going on and decide if I'm going to hold onto it for a while or remove it from my consciousness.

> "It is not sufficient to see and know the beauty of a work.
> We must feel and be affected by it."
> **Voltaire, eighteenth-century French
> writer and philosopher**

Tami acknowledges her own impulsivity.

My problem is impulsiveness. I get an idea or a feeling and instantly respond to it with little or no thought or consideration of consequences. After sixty-six years of life, you'd think I would have learned better control, but I haven't. I can't tell you how many times I've had to eat my words; how many times I've whimsically and irresponsibly lost a bunch of money; or how many times I've hurt someone or been hurt. Feelings are great, but I really need to remind myself to slow down and consider all of the facts and options before acting on my feelings.

Barbara, a dark-haired film editor, candidly admits.

From an early age, I was taught to experience my feelings and use them to learn more about myself. When I feel an internal change running through me, I treat it like most people would the sighting of a rainbow or a dolphin playing in the surf. I stop and let it take charge of me, totally experience it for a while, and then figure out what brought it on. I like that beginning part, where the emotion engulfs me and forces changes in my body. But I also like taking control back and forming a memory link that reminds me how I can avoid those feelings if I choose to or return to them if that's what I want.

"Our feelings are our most genuine paths to knowledge."

Audre Lorde, professor of literature and self-described "black lesbian, mother, warrior, poet"

Review

Feel with full awareness before analyzing or reacting and for as long as the feeling is productive.

❋

Self-Reflection

Mentally list the *feelings* that are easiest for you to connect with, those you infrequently experience, and those you'd like to be more in touch with.

Chapter 14

Love Yourself and Others

Why is LOVING important?

Love brings a depth and richness to life unmatched by any other emotion. It feels good, strengthens the immune system, and lengthens life. Love is nurturing and nourishing. It motivates you to be your best and inspires those around you to love more.

Love invites accompanying feelings of security, expansiveness, optimism, warmth, and connectedness. It heightens awareness and leads to a sense of being more in tune with your surroundings and in touch with yourself, others, and nature.

Experiencing life through feelings of love is invigorating, enriching, and reinforcing. It fortifies acceptance of who you are and how you're living, which leads to an even greater sense of security and appreciation of life.

The sense of security and hope derived from love allows you to approach life more boldly and creatively. It provides a space or environment in which you are empowered to try new things, explore, and experiment. Win or lose, you still love.

"You will find as you look back upon your life that the moments when you have really lived, are the moments when you have done things in a spirit of love."

Henry Drummond, late nineteenth-century Canadian poet and physician

How to Love

The journey of expanding your capacity to love begins with self-exploration. Consciously, consistently, proudly, and unapologetically acknowledge aspects of yourself you respect and in which you take pride and delight. For many, it's easier to recall and dwell on their personal shortcomings and mistakes than to identify and celebrate their strengths and successes. Work on changing that balance. Certainly you can go overboard in self-love. You can become self-involved, arrogant, and narcissistic. However, it does not make you an egocentric bore to simply identify those personal characteristics and abilities you hold in esteem. Each and every one of us has something to be proud of, to feel good about.

> "I began to understand that self-esteem isn't everything;
> it's just that there's nothing without it."
> **Gloria Steinem, writer best known for her support of the women's liberation movement**

As you grow in positive self-esteem and love, you have more to give. And as you give more, more is returned to you.

I love the twinkle in that old guy's eyes as he drives down the highway on his big chopper, gray ponytail trailing in the wind. Accept and love your ability to focus on the positive, lovable aspects of others, and you will be blessed by more and enhanced opportunities to love and feel loved.

Those clouds are gorgeous. The colors and smooth, graceful lines fill me with peace and joy. Accept and love your appreciation of life's gifts, and you will be blessed as life shares more of its bounties with you.

Grab the moment for love—don't take anything for granted. Even though you will probably be alive to enjoy many more days and years, there's a lot to be said for living each moment as if it were your last.

*Demand of yourself that every sight, sound, taste, touch, and feeling is deeply prized and cherished.

*Always be aware of and appreciate blessings.

*Make sure to take the time to connect, feel, and articulate your love for those close to you who are about to drive off to work or leave to run errands.

> "Wouldn't it be wonderful if we could all be a little more gentle with each other, and a little more loving, have a little more empathy, and maybe, we'd like each other a little bit more."
> **Judy Garland, American singer and motion picture actress**

If you knew today was your last day on earth, would you allow positive interactions with friends and family to go unappreciated? *No!* Would feelings of thanks and love go unexpressed? *No!* Would you give half of your attention to a life partner who was sharing something important and half to the ballgame on TV? *No!* Would a fond memory that stirs your heart be ignored? *No!* Love is a beautiful gift, one that should be embraced and appreciated at every opportunity.

There's something to love in every person you meet and every experience you encounter. Casually walking through the mall, driving in traffic, or sitting in a coffee shop, your development as a loving human being is vastly enhanced by diminishing or disregarding negative thoughts and feelings and focusing more on the positive.

I love watching that man take pride in his baby's babbling.

My heart is filled with joy when I see a mother and her daughter smiling and talking to each other.

Like him or hate him, you've got to love his dedication to the job. No one puts in the hours like Herb.

The more you limit negative thoughts and look for positive qualities and aspects to love in others, the more positive and loving you become and the more positive experiences and love will find you.

"Put love first.
Entertain thoughts that give life and when a thought or resentment, or hurt, or fear comes your way, have another thought that is more powerful—a thought that is love."
Mary Manin Morrissey, author, workshop leader, and spiritual guide

---

Examples of LOVING

Thin and drawn, yet exuding calm, peace, and joy, Neal discusses an unexpected gift his cancer bestowed upon him.

I'm sixty-one years old and praying to make it to sixty-two. Last year, when I was diagnosed with cancer, I learned the most important lesson of my life: love each day as if it is my last. I should have been living this way all along. I missed far too many special family events, neglected to express my love to a lot of people who really mattered to me, and fell way short of appreciating the blessings I had. Not anymore. When I hold my wife, I delight in the love that overwhelms me. When I visit or talk to my mom or kids, I never forget to focus on the positive and express my deep affection. People often say to me, "Oh my, cancer! I'm so sorry!" Well, most of the time, I'm not feeling sorry. My cancer has taught me to love and is helping me become a better person.

"You never lose by loving. You always lose by holding back."

Barbara DeAngelis, PhD, psychologist, author, and motivational speaker

Ting was given up for adoption soon after birth, but wasn't placed with a family until she was seven.

It took the first third of my sixty-four years on this earth to learn to value and love myself. It's hard when your parents give you away, and you start life in an orphanage and move to a home and town where everyone except you is Caucasian. It's hard, but my adoptive parents did a great job. They were always there for me with encouragement and support, accepted me for who I was, and loved me and taught me to love myself. The more I learned to accept and love myself, the more I was able to accept and love others.

Vance, an animated, smiling, seventy-one-year-old landscape designer recalls his upbringing.

My parents raised me to look for the good in everyone, to love and care for others as if they were my brothers and sisters. Sometimes I get taken advantage of because I'm so trusting and open and hardly ever look for or see the negative aspects of others. It happens, but I can live with that. I'd much rather spend my life seeing good and beauty and feeling love than the opposite. If you start not trusting, not caring, and not loving, just to protect yourself, you're making a big mistake.

"All that is necessary to make this world a better place to live in is to love..."
Isadora Duncan, American dancer and dance teacher

Review

Love yourself, others, and the world that surrounds you.

❁

Self-Reflection

Think back over the past week and recall the thoughts, experiences, and people who stimulated your deepest moments of *love*.

CHAPTER 15

GIVE WHAT YOU CAN GIVE

"Some people give time, some money, some their
skills and connections,
some literally give their life's blood. But everyone
has something to give."
Barbara Bush, popular first lady
and wife of the forty-first President of the United
States, George Herbert Walker Bush

Why is GIVING important?

Selfless, honest, heart-centered giving feels good. It brings an added sense of meaning and significance to life. Giving helps you connect with others in a positive way. It also benefits those who receive your giving and encourages them to give in their own ways, which makes your community and world a better place to live.

Giving reminds you that you're part of something greater than yourself and there's more in life than the accumulation of achievements, fortune, and fame.

Every act of giving benefits someone. Volunteering at a local school could help a child learn to read. Donating time to the neighborhood cleanup committee creates a more beautiful environment in which to live. Contributing thirty dollars to a charity may provide a Thanksgiving dinner for an impoverished family.

As the lives of those around you are improved, and their sense of appreciation is kindled, the possibility they will be encouraged to share that which they have in abundance is enhanced. Like a wave traveling across the sea, giving moves across a community, from one to the next to the next.

"When I give I give myself."
Walt Whitman, nineteenth-century American poet

How to GIVE

One important component of giving is leading a life consistent on the outside and inside. Open up and share who you are with those you come in contact with and, most importantly, with those you love and care for. Be and give to others your true and honest self.

Admire or look down upon me. Love or hate me. I respect you enough to be myself with you.

*Honey, sometimes I feel like I'm in over my head. I wonder if I really have what it takes to succeed in my new job.

*She can fire me if she wants, but I'm telling the boss what I really think about the proposed changes.

*My teenager thinks it's dumb and weird that I insist on saying "Good night" and telling her "I love you" every evening before bed, but she's dealt with it for seventeen years and will just have to deal with it as long as we live together.

> "It is not how much we give, but how much love we put in the giving."
> **Mother Teresa, Roman Catholic nun who received the 1979 Nobel Peace Prize**

As you progress in understanding and honestly sharing yourself, the likelihood increases that your giving will emanate from a desire to help the recipients rather than yourself; it will come from your heart rather than from a desire to satisfy your ego or personal need.

*Listening attentively to a forlorn acquaintance in order to get closer to him and gain some sort of advantage (e.g., power, money, sex) is not giving from the heart, whereas listening to help ease his pain is.

*You probably won't be a great Cub Scout or Brownie leader if you accept the responsibility simply because your company requires all employees to be involved in one civic organization. On the other hand, if your volunteer efforts are based on a love for and desire to help children, you'll almost certainly do a better job.

*You may collect the same amount of money fund-raising for a cause in order to further your social ambitions as you would fund-raising for a cause you strongly believe in, but the former will provide you with far less personal satisfaction.

> "In helping others, we shall help ourselves, for whatever good we give out completes the circle and comes back to us."
> **Flora Edwards, philanthropist and writer**

Make conscious decisions about where to direct your giving. No matter how much time or money you have, you can't give endlessly, nor can you meet the needs of everyone.

Others are often quite willing and eager to provide advice on where you should focus your efforts, but this is a decision that best comes from your own heart. The ideal targets should be people, causes, and organizations about which you care most deeply.

My husband thinks I should help coach our granddaughter's soccer team, but I don't like coaching. I'd much rather spend my free time helping in her classroom.

There's a lot of pressure on me to run for president of the club, but I dread the idea and would much rather work behind the scenes.

How much should you give? The ideal level is one that provides the most benefit to others without creating resentment or lack in your own life, or in the lives of those who mean the most to you. To do this well, be aware of how your giving affects you and those closest to you, and find a balance between that and your desire to help others.

Some seem able to give and give from an unending supply of time, energy, or money. Others struggle to keep their own lives together and appear to give very little. Most are somewhere in between. You must discover what is right for you.

> "If you haven't any charity in your heart, you have the worst kind of heart trouble."
> **Bob Hope, American comedian and actor**

Examples of GIVING

Until recently, it was all about me, states Helen, a divorced hairdresser in her early fifties.

I spent every dollar I earned and most of my free time indulging myself. My younger sister's husband passed away last year, and all that changed. I've been spending a lot of time and most of my discretionary earnings helping her out and doing special things and buying little presents for my niece and nephew. I never would have believed it, but I get a lot more pleasure spending fifty dollars taking them all out for dinner than I used to get going for a massage. And seeing the look on my niece's and nephew's faces when I bought them new sneakers was worth way more than the money I spent.

"No one has ever become poor by giving."
Anne Frank, a German-Jewish girl whose diary described her family's ordeal hiding from the Nazis in World War II.

Stan, who works many overtime hours to provide for his wife and elderly parents and help pay expenses for two sons in college, feels guilty about giving so little to his church.

I'd really like to donate more of my time and money to a couple of the wonderful projects our church is involved with, but working fifty or sixty hours a week, I just don't have the time, and I barely earn enough to pay the bills and put food on the table. Right now, it's all about supplying the basics for my family. When we have some extra money at the end of the month—and this doesn't happen a lot—my favorite "charity" is taking everyone out to a restaurant or a special family outing. That's just how it is now, so I'll live with a little bit of guilt until our situation changes.

Ria, a successful fifty-eight-year-old clothing designer, gives in a variety of ways.

My giving is really a mixed bag. To my husband, children, grandchildren, and parents, I give my time, attention, and love. They're at the top of my priority list. If and when they have a special event or need, I'm there. To my thirty-two employees, I give an excellent salary and ben-efits package, respect, encouragement, and gratitude. I don't give my time to any charities, but I do donate mon-ey to two organizations whose work I highly respect. In two or three years, my daughter will start managing the business, and I'll cut back to two or three days a week. When that happens, I plan on becoming more involved in community efforts to assist the poor and homeless and advocate for some global issues I care about.

> "I have found that among its other benefits, giving liberates the soul of the giver."
> **Maya Angelou, contemporary American author, poet, actress, and director**

Review

Give your true self to others; **give from the heart; give as much as you are able**.

✺

Self-Reflection

Make a mental accounting of your *giving* over the past week, whether it be through positive thoughts/prayers, words, time, possessions, or money.

CHAPTER 16

LET GO OF NONPRODUCTIVE THOUGHTS

"Holding on to anger, resentment and hurt only gives
you tense muscles,
a headache, and a sore jaw from clenching your teeth."
Joan Lunden, television journalist
and host of ABC-TV's
Good Morning America for almost two decades

Why is LETTING GO Important?

Letting go of recurring nonproductive thoughts relieves
your mind and body of a tremendous burden. When you
diminish thoughts of personal deficits, injustices suffered,

opportunities missed, the shortcomings of others, envy, jealousy, guilt...your mood is enhanced, the health of your cardiovascular and neurological systems is strengthened, and your attention for incoming information and sensations is increased.

Your time is much better spent enjoying an evening meal rather than mentally cursing the driver who cut you off in traffic; experiencing pride in your sister's accomplishments, as opposed to envying her new, luxury, beachfront house; and relishing life's possibilities instead of drowning in guilt over past shortcomings and future fears.

To make room for thoughts that will improve your life, let go of those that won't.

"The trick is not how much pain you feel but how much joy you feel.
Any idiot can feel pain. Life is full of excuses to feel pain,
excuses not to live; excuses, excuses, excuses."
Erica Jong, contemporary American novelist, much of whose work focuses on women's issues

---

How to LET GO

To let go successfully of recurring thoughts that pull you from living the moment and that lead you in negative, nonproductive directions, first become aware of them. Observe what your attention is focusing on and remind yourself you're in charge of this process. *Take charge* of your thoughts and how you respond to them. Ask yourself why in the world you allow your mind to repeat, over and over again, destructive mental musings like these:

He's such a lying, cheating ––!

Wrinkles and blotches. Wrinkles and blotches. My entire face is wrinkles and blotches.

I'll go nuts if she gives me one more responsibility.

By observing your mind's wanderings, you're more able to identify patterns of how you're thinking and thereby become better prepared to change focus.

How often do you think or speak critically of others, allow unwanted, negative emotions to weigh on you, or mentally rehash mistakes from the past? For most, simply becoming more aware of these occurrences is a productive first step.

> "Anger makes you smaller, while forgiveness forces you to grow beyond what you were."
> **Cherie Carter-Scott, PhD, author, talk-show host, and seminar leader**

Some negative thoughts that intrude on your consciousness do so as reminders or catalysts, encouraging you to confront people or issues that have not been resolved. When this is the case, the best way to let go is to deal with them.

I can't stop thinking this lump in my breast may be cancer. I'm having trouble concentrating and am always nervous. Check it out! See a physician. Get some tests.

Dave usually calls every weekend, but I haven't heard from him in three weeks. I wonder if he's upset with me? Give him a call. Write him an e-mail. Text him.

Whereas the thoughts in the previous examples should be dealt with before letting go, most negative thoughts can and should be quickly eliminated.

If I had kept that stock, I'd be a lot wealthier today. Let it go. Take the energy being wasted on looking back and put it to better use.

If it hadn't been for my lousy college advisor I'll bet I would have gone into a more appropriate career and wouldn't have spent thirty years hating my job. He ruined my life! Thoughts like this are of little value and are better discontinued and replaced with ones that are productive and nourishing.

> "Life is what we make it, always has been, always will be."
>
> **Grandma Moses, internationally renowned American folk artist who started painting in her seventies**

One of the best ways to eliminate these thoughts is to replace the negative with a positive. Two entities cannot exist in the same space at the same time. If you wish to let go of a negative thought, consistently replacing it with a positive thought puts you back in charge of your consciousness and gets you moving in a desirable direction.

LET GO OF NONPRODUCTIVE THOUGHTS 127

*Instead of thinking, *I want a cigarette. I need a ciga-rette. I was crazy to think I could give up smoking,* try thinking, *Deep breathing feels wonderfully invigorating and refreshing.*

*Instead of thinking, *I can't stand the stiffness and soreness in my neck and shoulders,* try thinking, *My back and knees feel great!*

Replacing the negative with a positive often works more efficiently when one, specific, positive thought or action is consistently linked or matched with a recurring negative one. Rather than allowing your consciousness to drift off freely and fixate on how those damn ––s are ruining the country, *take control* and switch your focus to tightening your stomach muscles or saying a silent prayer or visualizing the smiling faces and names of cousins. Replace the daily, or perhaps hourly, silent, "broken record" of resentment toward your boss's incompetence and poor people skills with trying to slow your heart beat or visualizing beautiful nature scenes or focusing on positive thoughts about your substantial salary and benefits or...

When you realize you're drifting toward the negative, switch over to the positive. The confidence and calm generated by the positive should, over time, reduce or possibly eliminate the occurrence of the negative.

"Reflect upon your present blessings, of which every man has plenty; not on your past misfortunes, of which all men have some."
Charles Dickens, nineteenth-century English novelist

Examples of LETTING GO

My dad fought in Europe during World War II, sixty-seven-year-old Nancy reports.

> *He vehemently hated Germans and everything German until just before he died. Whenever he heard a German accent or read anything related to Germany, you could see his body would tighten up, and he'd cuss under his breath. It wasn't until a few months before he died from lung cancer that he started mellowing out a little. The hospice worker taught Dad a technique. As soon as he became aware he was slipping into a hateful, angry place, he'd close his eyes and picture himself surrounded by his eight grandchildren. Those last few months were the most peaceful of his life. And they taught me a great lesson about letting go of thoughts and feelings that pull me down.*

"The hatred you're carrying is a live coal in your heart—far more damaging to yourself than to them."
Lawana Blackwell, contemporary American novelist

Annette, like millions of Americans, spends a few dollars each month on Powerball tickets.

> *I spend too much time thinking about all the things I'll buy when I win THE BIG ONE. One day, I got so involved with a fantasy, I didn't hear one word of my son's high-school graduation speech. It was one of the most significant events of his life, and I was*

there, in the audience, but my awareness was off at some luxury resort spending gobs of money. When the audience started applauding, and I realized what had happened, I swore to myself, "This has to stop." I'm trying a new approach to limit these nonproductive fantasies. As soon as I realize I've gone off into my millionaire dreamworld, I focus on my posture—shoulders back, stomach in, neck straight, chin parallel to the ground. For me, it works like a charm!

Phil, a fifty-one-year-old electrician, husband, and father, reluctantly admits his former fixation on his early evening beer.

I used to spend a lot of time at work imagining myself getting home and downing a couple of beers. The second I got home, I'd run right to the refrigerator, grab a cold one, and start drinking. Last year, my wife suggested I wasn't being a good role model for our teenage son and daughter. At first I thought she was nuts. What's the big deal if I have a couple or three beers? But the more I thought about it, the more I saw her point. I got this idea of replacing beer with water. Now, if I think about beer during the day, I immediately change my mental image from beer to a huge bottle of water. As soon as I get home, I grab a quart bottle of no calorie, strawberry-flavored water—I always have a bunch lined up in the fridge— and drink it right down. An after-work strawberry water has replaced my two or three beers. My wife is happy, the kids have a better role model, and I've lost ten pounds.

> "To get what you want, STOP doing
> what isn't working."
> **Dennis Weaver, television actor,
> environmentalist, and author**

Summary

*LET GO by **becoming aware of where your thoughts are leading you** and **making a conscious decision to change—replace negatives with positives**.*

❁

Self-Reflection

For the next hour, observe each time a critical or negative thought crosses your mind.

Chapter 17

QUESTION and Find Answers

Why is QUESTIONING important?

Questioning that which you do not understand leads to learning. Questioning when something doesn't seem quite right helps avoid mistakes and diminishes disagreement with others. Questioning with an open mind, with the desire and willingness to understand and the flexibility to change beliefs and actions, indicates you value responses and encourages those being questioned to share.

Information, knowledge, and truth rarely just drop in your lap. You need to search them out.

When questions are focused inwardly (*how can I best balance work, family, and taking care of myself?*), they lead to a clearer understanding of self; when focused on learning about and helping others (*you seem upset; what's going on?*), they lead to closer, more caring and connected relationships.

When asking questions that help you learn, clarify, and connect with others, you expand your intellect, understanding of the world, and ability to function efficiently, cooperatively, and joyously in society.

> "Once you start to question your life you get to a higher level of awareness.
> It's like turning on a light..."
> **Naomi Judd, country singer, songwriter,**
> **and American Liver Foundation spokesperson**

How to QUESTION

The primary goal of questioning is to learn: to acquire data and attain understanding. To do this, recognize when you need more information, and be bold enough to expect and demand that your questions are answered sufficiently.

Every day, numerous situations arise in which you don't have one-tenth of the information needed to truly understand what's going on, but you don't really need to. On the other hand, there are many situations in which you really do need to understand, and, therefore, you must slow down, ask questions, and gather more information.

*A sad or angry expression on the face of a stranger can easily be ignored; however, the same expression on the face of a husband or wife begs attention.

*A casual acquaintance's comment about her son's failing marriage may not lead you on a quest for further information, whereas your daughter's statement that she and her husband are having some problems will no doubt prompt you to delve more deeply.

Once the need to know more becomes apparent, be bold, and sometimes even aggressive, in searching out information. If a response doesn't seem correct or complete, you can ask direct questions (*how, what, where, why, when*).

*Your partner dismissively saying that he will get over it and that you shouldn't worry probably needs to be further investigated. *What happened? How can I help?*

*Your daughter sharing that she and her husband argue all the time, over every little thing, demands that you seek more information. *How do the arguments usually start? What process do you use to come to agreements?*

> ## "If you don't ask, you don't get."
> **Stevie Wonder, American composer,**
> **singer, and musician**

You can also gather information without a direct question, by expressing your uncertainty or inner conflict.

I'd really like to understand what you're going through.

I've never seen you two fight about anything. I thought everything was going great between you.

Far too many communications are not clear and open because individuals ignore the faint voices in their heads that say, *Something's not right...The whole picture isn't clear...I need to know more.* These urgings need to be heeded. You don't want to be obnoxious and overly pushy, yet you shouldn't be satisfied with insufficient responses.

In order to ensure that you receive the most accurate information possible, your questions are best directed to the most knowledgeable and reliable sources available. If your wife (or husband or son or daughter) is upset, talking with her (or him) is usually a much better approach than talking to someone else about her (or him). If you're uncertain about whether or not Medicare will pay for new orthotics, your podiatrist is a better resource than a friend who wears orthotics.

Employ these basic techniques as you question: remain sensitive and civil; allow individuals the opportunity to express themselves without interruption; demonstrate with eye contact and body language that you are attentive and interested; and occasionally rephrase or paraphrase what you've heard to make sure your understanding is correct.

You may think you have the answer, but it's possible you don't. Perhaps you asked the wrong question or worded it unclearly or the person you asked heard something different from what you intended or you agreed but didn't clarify the details, and you both left with different pictures in mind. Listen with open ears and an open mind, valuing the communications of others, and trying to understand as much as you can.

Question and clarify. Question and learn. Question and reassure yourself that what you believe is true.

> "The real questions...make your mind start vibrating like a jackhammer;
> the ones that you 'come to terms with' only to discover that they are still there...
> they barge into your life at the times when it seems most important for them to stay away."
>
> **Ingrid Bengis, Russian-born American writer and business entrepreneur**

Examples of QUESTIONING

Gray-haired, with beautiful, clear, brown eyes, Valerie obviously loves discussing her marriage.

Every year, on or near our wedding anniversary, my husband and I go to a quiet restaurant or bar, order drinks, and discuss a list of ten questions we wrote forty years ago. Some of the questions are just about us, about how we're doing in different aspects of our lives, whereas some relate to our relationship. First, we evaluate how we did on what we wrote the previous year. Then, we separately write new goals and plans for each question. Finally, we read our answers to each other and talk about them. I can't imagine an anniversary passing without doing this. If you don't ask the questions, I think you run the risk of stagnating.

"If we would have new knowledge, we must get a whole world of new questions."

Susanne K. Langer, twentieth-century American philosopher, writer, and teacher

---

Marty, a fifty-one-year-old accountant, who works in a large corporation's central office, is mad at himself for not asking more questions sooner.

Fifteen years I spent with that company, hoping to make my way up the corporate ladder. Finally, I went to my division head and asked, "Why do I keep getting passed over?" His response shocked me! "Marty, we think you do OK in your position, but no one on the executive team sees you succeeding at a higher level." As I questioned him further, I learned I could have gotten the same answers ten or twelve years earlier. They had a pretty good idea from the start that I wasn't going to move up. All those years of wonder, doubt, and anxiety could have been avoided if I had just asked the question sooner.

"The fool wonders, the wise man asks."

Benjamin Disraeli, first Jewish Prime Minister of Great Britain (1868 and 1874–1880)

Whitney, a successful marriage counselor, has definite opinions about how partners need to communicate to keep a marriage fresh and alive.

A lot of what I do is teach partners to be better communicators—to ask questions and really listen to responses. So many people don't listen. Sometimes partners will say, "How was your day?" and then start reading the newspaper or daydreaming when the other person begins to answer. They'll jump in now and again with off-the-wall, unrelated questions. They try to make it seem like they're listening, but they really aren't. Communicating like that doesn't fool anyone and tends to build an even greater separation or wall between partners.

"Don't spend your precious time asking 'Why isn't this world a better place?'
It will only be time wasted. The question to ask is 'How can I make it better?'
To that there is an answer."

Leo Buscaglia, PhD, professor, motivational speaker, and self-help author

Review

Boldly question the right people or sources with an **open mind** and **true desire to know and understand**.

❀

Self-Reflection

Recall the last time you assumed you understood a communication, but really didn't, and a problem arose. What might you have done differently?

Chapter 18

ORGANIZE the Details of Life

"Organizing is what you do before you do
something,
so that when you do it, it is not all mixed up."
A. A. Milne, author of *Winnie-the-Pooh*

Why is ORGANIZING important?

Improved organization of schedules and environments yields a calmer, more relaxed, less distracted existence. These changes lead to you completing more tasks, enhanced results from your efforts, an increase in discretionary time, and a boost in mental and physical energy. As the arrangement and systematization of schedules and environments improves, you find yourself less often losing things, rushing around, being late, missing important events, and falling short of expectations and potential.

Being organized also makes you better prepared to handle new, incoming tasks and to respond quickly to situations and surprises. Organizationally challenged individuals often find themselves unprepared for and overwhelmed by additional responsibilities, which can't be easily assimilated into an already frenetic, overtaxed, and confusing schedule or system. A new job has to vie for attention and time with a myriad of already existing, challenging projects. Something's got to give. What often gets shortchanged are critical components of a well-balanced life, such as spending time with family and friends, making it to exercise class, getting enough sleep, eating properly, participation in leisure activities, and preparing for the future.

> "Good order is the foundation of all things."
> **Edmund Burke, eighteenth-century British statesman and author**

How to ORGANIZE

Critical components in sound organization are a place or procedure for everything, and everything in its place or following procedure. It's straightforward, easy, and doesn't take much time to initiate. First, create the plan, system, or routine, and then adhere to it. Your goal is to deal quickly and consistently with the countless small tasks that face you every day. Following this approach creates a greater sense of satisfaction, enhanced mental peace, and additional discretionary time to engage in the nonroutine aspects of life. You need both the system and consistent adherence to the system.

The best way to begin to implement a place or procedure for everything and everything in its place or following procedure is with your most simple, recurring, annoying problem spots.

*If you habitually waste minutes each day searching for keys, select a specific place to keep them.

*Instead of suffering the frustration of being unable to remember usernames and passwords you've created, keep some type of secure, perhaps coded, master list you can easily access.

These aren't *the* solutions; they're *sample* solutions— examples of how a little order or a logical procedure might help.

You may have a place or procedure for everything, yet still struggle to keep everything in its place or following a procedure.

*The file cabinet in your office is well organized and labeled, yet you place papers in stacks, on the floor, and along the side of the wall.

*Your calendar is diligently kept up to date; however, you don't refer to it often enough and frequently miss appointments and forget to follow through on commitments and intentions.

Using the systems you design requires discipline. It requires that you don't put off for later what can be done right away. You have to, at times, allow and coerce your organized, responsible, ego-parent-self to enforce the rules, and make your less-organized, less-responsible, id-child-self *do it*: take three seconds to write *eggs* on the shopping list; pull open the file drawer and deposit last month's phone bill where it belongs; refer to your schedule throughout the day so that you go where you're supposed to go and do what you're supposed to do.

"Failing to plan is planning to fail."
**Effie Jones, teacher and school administrator
who organized the Office of Minority Affairs at the
American Association of School Administrators**

Another important component of sound organization is focusing on priorities. When organizing your world, keep the most important engagements and responsibilities clearly in mind.

*The report needs another proofing and some changes; however, that will have to wait. I don't want to be late for my two o'clock meeting.

*I'd rather not work out in the morning, but I'd better today because if I do my normal afternoon workout, I run the risk of not getting Dad to his physical therapy session on time.

*I'd like to stand here talking to Sally for ten more minutes, but then I'd be late for my afternoon appointment.

> "The key is not to prioritize what's on your schedule but to schedule your priorities."
> **Dr. Stephen R. Covey, leadership and management expert and author of** *The 7 Habits of Highly Effective People*

Finally, regularly check your to-do lists and make sure sufficient progress is being made. Many find it helpful to do this in writing—make a list, from most important to least or from morning to afternoon to evening, and check off items as they're accomplished. This is a particularly useful approach for individuals who have ADHD, suffer from memory difficulties, and the elderly (hopefully not us, *yet!*), all of whom are at risk for organizational challenges.

> "I see something that has to be done, and I organize it."
> **Elinor Guggenheimer, eminent twentieth-century New York City civic leader and activist**

Examples of ORGANIZING

Until a few months ago, Bernie, a short, plump, sociable sixty-three-year-old, hated his new job selling insurance.

People were always getting mad at me for being slow and missing deadlines. My boss blew up one day and said, "This is your last chance! When you have a call to make or papers to get signed, you have to do it right away. No more I'll-get-to-it-when-I-get-to-it attitude." That really shook me up. I started keeping two different lists, one that had to be finished each day before I went home and the other of things to be finished by noon on Saturday. The system changed my life. I'm working the same number of hours as I used to, but I'm much more efficient. For the past three months, I've issued more new policies than anyone else in the company and love my job.

> "Look at a day when you are supremely
> satisfied at the end.
> It's not a day when you lounge
> around doing nothing;
> it's when you've had everything to
> do, and you've done it."
> **Margaret Thatcher, first female prime minister of
> Great Britain (1979–1990)**

Anna, a fifty-seven-year-old university English professor, found that good organization gave her more time to pursue a dream.

I used to give everything to my teaching, advising, and committee work, and very little to writing. My passion has always been writing, but there never seemed to be any time. Last year, I reorganized my schedule and set aside Monday, Wednesday, and Friday mornings to work on a novel I started years ago but never finished. I plan the rest of my week around those times and never let anything interfere. The quality of my teaching, advising, and committee work has remained the same, yet I'm making great progress on the book. My new schedule has made me a lot more efficient.

"Don't agonize. Organize."
Florynce Kennedy, twentieth-century American lawyer and political activist

---

Gordon, a sixty-two-year-old marketing executive, found that organization saved him time.

My desk used to be piled with stacks of papers. There was no space to write, rest my elbow, or put a cup of coffee. I couldn't find anything. One day, I heard an organization expert on the radio say, "More than 80 percent of the paper that comes our way should be glanced at and dropped directly into the recycle bin; 10 percent should be filed away; and another 10 percent should be dealt with immediately or placed in a priority folder, which is never allowed to get fatter than one inch." I started the system immediately. It's amazing how much time I now save and how my desk has turned into an ally rather than an enemy.

Review

Focus on priorities as you organize your time and things with **a place or procedure for everything** and **everything in its place or following a procedure**.

※

Self-Reflection

Under the general umbrella of organization, what are your greatest strengths and most significant challenges?

CHAPTER 19

VARY PERSPECTIVES, HABITS, INTERESTS, AND SURROUNDINGS

"Twenty years from now you will be more
disappointed by the things that you didn't do than by
the ones you did do. So...Explore. Dream. Discover."
Mark Twain, major American author of the
nineteenth-century

Why is VARYING important?

Varying habits and interests exposes you to a wider variety of experiences and aspects of your personal potential; helps you avoid the stress and strain that sometimes accompanies hyperfocus or overuse; allows you to learn more about the rich smorgasbord of life that surrounds you; and exercises, enriches, and expands the connections between areas of your brain.

Varying the people you spend time with and the environments you spend time in creates opportunities to broaden your education and understanding, options for how to live your life, and appreciation for what you have.

Varying perspectives, the angle from which you analyze issues and situations, increases your sensitivity to and understanding of other points of view, heightens perceptions, expands analytical skills and abilities to creatively search for solutions, and broadens opportunities to communicate openly with and become closer to others.

Varying the cultural events you attend, the sports and exercises you participate in, the entertainment you expose yourself to, the trips you take, and the books you read brings a broader perspective and balance to your life and nourishes your creative, discovering, expanding nature.

> "A person needs at intervals to separate from family and companions and go to new places. One must go without familiars in order to be open to influences, to change."
> **Katharine Butler Hathaway, American author who lived for many years in Paris and traveled the world despite a serious, disabling spinal condition**

How to VARY

The first step in the varying process is relaxing or quieting the tied-to-routine parts of your brain, thereby allowing yourself to consider, be exposed to, and gain from a wider variety of experiences, points of view, and people. On occasion, step outside of established habits and interests and try something new. You don't have to give up preferences, beliefs, or opinions; however, if you become imprisoned by them, your ability to grow, learn, change, and adapt becomes limited.

> "You must learn day to day, year by year, to broaden your horizon.
> The more things you love, the more you are interested in,
> the more you are indignant about,
> the more you have left when anything happens."
> **Ethel Barrymore, American stage and motion-picture star of the early twentieth-century**

As you allow yourself to experience and appreciate a wider variety of life's many hidden treasures, consider these two guidelines for safe varying:

1. Start with small steps; and
2. Remain true to your core beliefs and long-term goals.

Start with small steps because the objective is not to turn your entire life around or remake yourself. The idea behind *varying* is to widen perspectives, to open up, to extend your comfort zones.

I don't like spinach, haven't had a bite since I was five years old. Come on! Consider taking one little bite of spinach lasagna or a spinach casserole. People far too often formulate strong preferences and dislikes at very early ages, unnecessarily limiting themselves. Does it make sense to allow who you were at five, six, or seven years old to dominate your interactions with the world at fifty, sixty, or seventy?

I believe in capital punishment. Anyone who doesn't is stupid or blind. Fine, believe in capital punishment. However, how about listening to the other side of the issue and identifying one anti-capital punishment point that seems reasonable?

"If we don't change, we don't grow.
If we don't grow, we aren't really living."
Gail Sheehy, self-help author and *Vanity Fair*
contributing editor

The best places to start taking these small steps are in behaviors or areas of your life where you don't know why you behave in a certain way or don't have strong beliefs to support your behavior.

*Not attending a concert because you feel uncomfortable in large crowds is more easily justified than not attending because you went to see the Beatles forty years ago and had trouble parking and could barely see the stage from your balcony seats.

*Avoiding jazz clubs is a very different issue for an alcoholic who's trying to stay sober than for someone who doesn't want to go because he or she has never been before.

When you do possess a core belief or long-term goal upon which a behavior or attitude is based, the recommendation to *vary* should be followed very cautiously, if at all.

*The man who gains great peace and fulfillment from praying every morning is ill-advised to vary his routine without good reason. But if morning prayer is unfulfilling and based solely on habit or guilt, perhaps a little variation (e.g., praying at another time of day, in a different location, or looking into some other spiritual practice) might be a good idea.

*The woman who loves oil painting and has dedicated her leisure hours to creating a completed canvas each month, with the goal of a public show in thirty months, is most probably engaged in a fulfilling and valuable endeavor. Even though varying may be needed at some time, to rest body parts, maintain interest, or see to other life requirements, it may not be necessary.

The recommendation to vary experiences, points of view, and people with whom you interact is not an invitation to have an affair, discard an old friendship, experiment with drugs, or steal a candy bar from the local supermarket; it's an invitation to explore positive ways to make your life more exciting, creative, open, and fulfilling.

"They say that time changes things, but you actually have to change them yourself."
Andy Warhol, American artist and leader of the Pop Art movement of the 1930s

Examples of VARYING

Throughout my late twenties, thirties, and early forties, I was super into weightlifting, fifty-three-year-old Joe admits.

I had huge muscles, but my belly was as big as my chest, and I couldn't touch my toes or run more than a few seconds without huffing and puffing. When I started developing back trouble, I realized there was more to good health than big muscles. Now I complement weight training with stretching, and using the exercise bicycle and treadmill. The results have been great. My weight is down, flexibility up, back pain diminished, and cardiovascular health dramatically improved. Like everything else in life, too much of a good thing may not be all that good.

"If you have always done it that way, it is probably wrong."
Charles Kettering, holder of more than two hundred patents and founder of the
Charles F. Kettering Foundation, which sponsors scientific research for the benefit of humanity

---

Franz, a sixty-seven-year-old widower, excitedly reveals how changing his perspective changed his relationship.

I took an adult-education psychology class last year and picked up this great technique to help me better understand and communicate with people. I have these make-believe, two-way conversations, where I play both parts. Sometimes I just do it in my mind, or by turning my head one direction and then the other, but sometimes I physically move from one chair to another and talk and make facial expressions like two different people. (Sounds strange, I know. But it really helps!) When I get into the role of the other person, I feel him and understand him much better. I've expanded the technique and use it with my girlfriend. She pretends to be me, and I pretend to be her. It really helps us understand each other better and work through issues more openly and quickly.

Karen fondly recalls her family's yearly summer vacation.

For many years, my husband, C. J., our sons, grandkids, and I spent a few days at Bass Lake every summer. We loved it there, but the boys, their wives, and I wanted to try some other places. C. J. was real resistant. We continued going to Bass Lake the next two years, but it wasn't the same. Finally, we convinced C. J. to try a campground on the Snake River. We all loved it. We did the Snake three years in a row. Just last year we all agreed it was time to return to Bass Lake, and we had the best time ever. I think it's great to change what you do now and again—it's interesting and also helps you appreciate what you've got when you go back.

"A well-rounded life is like a safety net under you. It allows you to do fancier tricks on the high wire."

Jane Pauley, news reporter and long-time broadcaster for NBC's *Today Show*

Summary

***Vary perspectives, habits, interests, surroundings,** and the **people you relate with**.*

❊

Self-Reflection

On each of the subtopics of *varying* highlighted in the *summary*, how are you different now from twenty-five years ago?

Chapter 20

RENEW Yourself and Your Relationships

"We must always change, renew, rejuvenate
ourselves; otherwise we harden."
Goethe, eighteenth- to nineteenth-century German
poet, novelist, and playwright

Why is RENEWING important?

The trials and tribulations of everyday life can cause serious wear and tear on your being, unless special attention is paid to personal renewal. With a focused effort to counteract drains and strains, the chances are dramatically enhanced that the passing years will bless you with diminished stress, a deeper understanding of self and your place in the universe, continuously improving professional skills, closer relationships with loved ones, and fewer health concerns than might otherwise have occurred.

No matter your age, you can reach and surpass goals and continue to mature and develop as a son or daughter, mother or father, friend, artist, worker, spiritual being, and thinker. Imagine how wonderfully life-affirming it would be to more often hear comments such as these:

Marriage counseling helped us work out a lot of issues that had been building for years. We've never been more in love or happier.

I took my whole vacation this year and came back energized and excited. It's amazing how a couple of weeks away can make such a difference.

Few aspects of life remain unchanged over time. The surest path to making those changes positive is the path of personal renewal.

> "Every now and then go away,
> have a little relaxation,
> for when you come back to your
> work your judgment will be surer.
> Go some distance away because then
> the work appears smaller
> and more of it can be taken in at a glance
> and a lack of harmony and proportion
> is more readily seen."
> **Leonardo Da Vinci, Italian Renaissance
> painter and inventor**

How to RENEW

Let's begin with your body, the capsule you inhabit. Good physical health requires constant vigilance. Make sure you have the following in your daily life:

*Regular exercise, to maintain weight, muscle strength, flexibility, and cardiovascular fitness.

*Proper diet, to nourish your body, fight off disease, and supply you with energy.

*Adequate relaxation and sleep, to rest and replenish all systems.

*Deep, rhythmic breathing, to provide oxygen for optimal brain and body functioning.

All must be attended to, regularly and thoughtfully. Each, in its own way, renews and makes you better prepared to face life.

"Put duties aside at least an hour before bed and perform soothing, quiet activities that will help you relax."
Dianne Hales, medical journalist and health and fitness author

---

Whereas maintaining a healthy body is important, of equal, or perhaps even greater importance is taking care of your psychological and spiritual health. When life pulls you down, do something to combat it. Act, rest, run, pray, play; take ten minutes and close your eyes; or spend ten days on a beach or mountaintop.

> "Walk away from it until you're stronger. All your problems will be there when you get back, but you'll be better able to cope."
> **Lady Bird Johnson, founder of the** *National Wildflower Research Center* **and wife of the thirty-sixth president of the United States, Lyndon Baines Johnson**

Another positive and efficient method of psychological renewal is to analyze or discuss with a friend or counselor what's going on in your mind, and if a change seems like a good idea, determine what approaches you could employ.

I keep fantasizing about walking away from my job and living off my savings while I write a book. Does that sound ridiculous, or do you think there's some value to the idea?

I've felt so useless and lethargic since the kids went away to college. How are you dealing with your empty-nest adjustment?

Sometimes you may need to establish or reaffirm and replenish connectedness with values, ideals, and powers greater than yourself.

I need to get back into volunteering at the animal shelter.

I want to pray more.

I value honesty and openness, yet I hide so much. I need to let it out.

Connecting in this way provides many people with a constant and significant source of renewal.

For most, an important component of psychological and spiritual health is relationships: caring about and being cared for, helping and being helped, loving and being loved. The web of loved ones with whom your life is intertwined can provide an abundant source of physical, psychological, and spiritual nutrition.

It doesn't take a lot to maintain or renew these relationships. A hug, loving glance, telephone call, word of encouragement, card or letter, or a few minutes of your attention can bring you closer together. It doesn't take all that much time to demonstrate to others that you care and want to be closer to them.

As people approach the end of life, few wish they had shared less time and love with family or friends or been less involved with and thoughtful toward work associates and acquaintances. Most often, the opposite is closer to the truth.

Besides renewing your physical, psychological, and spiritual self, and relationships with others, you should also consider your work and make every effort to seek continued growth there as well. No matter how competent a receptionist, attorney, coach, maintenance worker, or police officer you are, you can be better. This can be accomplished through reflective practice, reading, classes, observing others, asking for and responding to feedback, or any one of a dozen other approaches. The personal and professional gains derived from improving your skills almost always outweigh the required investment of time or money. The key is to continue to grow, to improve.

> "Inside myself is a place where I live all alone and that's where you renew your springs that never dry up."
> **Pearl S. Buck, American author who won the 1938 Nobel Prize for literature**

Examples of RENEWING

Sam, who appears younger than his fifty-six years, is a sales representative for a large, international company.

I could work twenty-four-seven and still not reach half the market I'd like to. If I didn't pay diligent, focused attention to keeping balanced, I'm sure I'd have burnt out years ago. I need seven hours of sleep and get it. I exercise every day, even if it means walking up and down the stairs in my hotel or doing calisthenics in my room. I communicate regularly with family and my closest friends. And I sketch, mostly people's faces and expressions, for at least ten or fifteen minutes a day. If I don't do these things, all of them, I don't do my job as well and am not as happy.

Chelsea, an assistant manager of a shopping mall, honestly shares a personal need.

It's hard for me to get any quiet time. With two energetic teenagers and a husband who's always playing with a garage full of tools and motorized vehicles, my home is one noisy place. I spend eight hours a day in a busy shopping mall supervising fifty employees, answering questions, and dealing with problems. When five o'clock comes, I need peace and quiet. On my way home, I stop at the YMCA and head straight to the stretching room. I just take off my shoes and lie there on a soft mat, breathing and stretching. I usually need only twenty minutes to drain all the noise and tension out and feel restored.

> ## "Spending quiet time alone gives your mind an opportunity to renew itself and create order."
> **Susan Taylor Brown, children's author and workshop presenter**

Isaac, a sixty-four-year-old electric company employee, is just coming out of a difficult period in his life.

My wife always made sure I talked to my parents, sisters, and friends at least once a week. And she scheduled my time with the kids and grandkids and encouraged me to do fun things with them. After our divorce, I grew distant from everyone and had trouble with depression. It took a few months for me to figure out what was going on. It was up to me to keep in touch with people I cared about. I found the more time I spent working on these relationships, the less depressed I felt. I began to understand that it takes time, energy, and commitment to keep my life in balance.

> "So as long as a person is capable of self-renewal, they are a living being."
> **Henri Frederic Amiel, nineteenth-century Swiss philosopher and poet**

Review

Renew yourself physically, psychologically, professionally, and **spiritually, as well as your relationships** with family, friends, and coworkers.

❋

Self-Reflection

Are your *renewal* efforts evenly spread over the five areas highlighted above or are certain aspects getting more or less of your attention?

CONCLUSION

I hope you've enjoyed reading *The Boomers' Guidebook to More Joyous Living—Twenty Positive Approaches to Life after Fifty* and that it has stimulated your desire to take an even more focused and assertive command over who you are becoming.

E. M. Forester, twentieth-century British author of *A Room with a View* and *A Passage to India* wrote, "The only books that influence us are those for which we are ready, and which have gone a little farther down our particular path than we have yet gone ourselves." Whereas you were motivated to select and read *The Boomers' Guidebook*, I'm hoping I was able to have a positive influence on your "particular path."

Based on Forester's quote, you probably were influenced the most by those approaches you are already quite proficient at and have naturally been implementing for decades. In my life experience, *playing, exercising, celebrating, negotiating, aiming toward goals, daring, upgrading, starting, working, feeling, questioning, organizing, varying*, and *renewing* have always been instinctive, almost effortless areas of strength. They're part of my DNA. Which of the *twenty positive approaches* are more established and built-in to *your* hard-drive? Take a moment and celebrate how fortunate you are to possess these characteristics and positive habits.

A number of the *twenty approaches* have required and continue to require a lot more of my attention in order to advance. The same is probably true for you, too. These areas are where our real work lies, where a greater focus and years of effort will make a significant, positive difference. I continue to challenge myself to improve the quality of my *breathing, meditating, positive influence over myself and others, loving, giving,* and *letting-go of negative thoughts.* Take a moment to remind yourself what you want or need to work on. Whereas awareness is a necessary and positive step in our process of change, celebrate your newfound awareness.

Your next step, our next step, is happening right now, this moment. Stay in tune with your breath, body, and where your thoughts are leading you, and listen to and watch your words, actions, and interactions with others. Share thoughts and feelings with loved ones, work at work worth doing, and continue the never-ending, always exciting, profoundly growth-producing path of self-discovery.

I want to wish you good luck on your path. Do your best. Keep moving in a positive direction. And don't kick yourself when something doesn't go as hoped. May your journey be shweet (my favorite, made up word).

Please visit my website at *TheBoomersGuidebook. com* for information on related workshops and inservice trainings.

Most sincerely,

Don Weinhouse

9 781490 433745